PRAISE FOR *ANX*

"I love Max Lucado and I love his new book, *Anxious for Nothing*. Scripture is so clear on the topic of worry, and Max has beautifully, and accessibly, laid out a plan for dealing with the stress that can rule, and ruin, our lives."
— ANDY STANLEY, PASTOR, AUTHOR, COMMUNICATOR, AND FOUNDER OF NORTH POINT MINISTRIES

"*Anxious for Nothing* is a profound and prophetic message for everyone in these chaotic times. Max reminds us that we can trust God in all things. He is good, he does good, and he is working all things together for your good and His Glory. Fear, terror, and uncertainty cripple so many, this book will help you to step into the future with faith and hope."
— CHRISTINE CAINE, FOUNDER OF A21 AND PROPEL WOMEN

"Okay, I'll admit it. Every Easter I still pull out *No Wonder They Call Him Savior*, just to see if there's an illustration I can use for my Easter message! Max Lucado is one of the most prolific and powerful storytellers of our time. When I read his latest book, *Anxious For Nothing*, the line that leaped off the page at me was, 'You can be the air traffic controller of your mental airport. You occupy the control tower and can direct the mental traffic of your world!' BOOM! Only Max can write like that. Please read this book from cover to cover. You don't want to miss a word!"
— RICH WILKERSON, LEAD PASTOR, TRINITY CHURCH, MIAMI, FLORIDA

"In a world filled with fear and anxiety, bestselling author Max Lucado reminds us of the inner peace that transcends the chaos. A must-read, as you navigate the noise of daily living."
— A. R. BERNARD

" 'Hi, I'm Dave, and I am a chronic worrier.' (Hi Dave.) Worry truly has been a struggle for me to overcome. The book of Philippians has helped me keep this beast at bay. And reading *Anxious for Nothing* is teaching me how to paralyze the potency of life's worries. Thanks, Max, for pointing us to the One who is stronger than our circumstances, bigger than our problems, and able to give us peace each day."
— DAVE STONE, SENIOR PASTOR, SOUTHEAST CHRISTIAN CHURCH, LOUISVILLE, KENTUCKY

"Despite decades of success as a writer and teacher, Max Lucado never settles for simply going through the motions. He always meets readers right where they are. In *Anxious for Nothing*, Max acknowledges the power of anxiety but also reminds us that there is hope to overcome it."

—DAVE RAMSEY, BESTSELLING AUTHOR AND
   NATIONALLY SYNDICATED RADIO SHOW HOST

"Wouldn't it be great to live a life without fear? How about living a life without anxiety? The good news is that it is possible and the answer is in the Word of God. In his new book, *Anxious for Nothing*, Max Lucado uses scripture to explain how you can take a stand against anxiety, worry, and fear and live a life filled with hope, peace, and faith."

—ROBERT MORRIS, FOUNDING SENIOR PASTOR, GATEWAY CHURCH,
   DALLAS/FORT WORTH, TEXAS; BESTSELLING AUTHOR OF *THE BLESSED
   LIFE*, *THE GOD I NEVER KNEW*, *TRULY FREE*, AND *FREQUENCY*

" 'Be not afraid nor dismayed . . .' was the Lord's personal word to Joshua. Though already assured of victory, his heart was still fretfully human. Your heart, too, might be trembling today. God has a personal word for you. Max puts it into plain view and makes it easy to understand. It will encourage you."

—PASTOR CARTER CONLON, SENIOR PASTOR, TIMES SQUARE CHURCH, NYC;
   AUTHOR OF *FEAR NOT: LIVING COURAGEOUSLY IN UNCERTAIN TIMES*

"Anxiety never plays favorites. That's why every person in every stage of life needs some practical help to identify—and overcome—its devastating power. Max's biblical approach provides the tools you need to regain control of your life and bring a sense of calm to the chaos inside."

—CHRIS BROWN, FINANCIAL EXPERT, PASTOR AND
   SPEAKER FOR RAMSEY SOLUTIONS

"Pastor Max Lucado has a way with words that graciously invites each and every one of us in to his living room for an honest and Christ-centered conversation about the Word of God. This book is all that and more—addressing a topic that affects us all. He will pastorally and strategically lead you to victory and freedom over what he describes as the war on worry."

—BOBBIE HOUSTON, GLOBAL CO-SENIOR PASTOR OF HILLSONG CHURCH

"Worry tries to grab all of us and hold us tight, but Max Lucado offers real steps and genuine truth to help us get out of the grasp of anxiety and live a more peaceful life."

—ANNIE F. DOWNS, BESTSELLING AUTHOR OF *LOOKING
   FOR LOVELY* AND *LET'S ALL BE BRAVE*

anxious

for

NOTHING

ALSO BY MAX LUCADO

INSPIRATIONAL

3:16
A Gentle Thunder
A Love Worth Giving
And the Angels Were Silent
Anxious for Nothing
Because of Bethlehem
Before Amen
Come Thirsty
Cure for the Common Life
Facing Your Giants
Fearless
Glory Days
God Came Near
Grace
Great Day Every Day
He Chose the Nails
He Still Moves Stones
How Happiness Happens
In the Eye of the Storm
In the Grip of Grace
It's Not About Me
Just Like Jesus
Max on Life
More to Your Story
Next Door Savior
No Wonder They Call Him the Savior
On the Anvil
Outlive Your Life
Six Hours One Friday
The Applause of Heaven
The Great House of God
Traveling Light
Unshakable Hope
When Christ Comes
When God Whispers Your Name
You'll Get Through This

FICTION

Christmas Stories
Miracle at the Higher Grounds Café
The Christmas Candle

BIBLES (GENERAL EDITOR)

Children's Daily Devotional Bible
Grace for the Moment Daily Bible
The Lucado Life Lessons Study Bible

CHILDREN'S BOOKS

A Max Lucado Children's Treasury
Do You Know I Love You, God?
God Always Keeps His Promises
God Forgives Me, and I Forgive You
God Listens When I Pray
Grace for the Moment: 365 Devotions for Kids
Hermie, a Common Caterpillar
I'm Not a Scaredy Cat
Itsy Bitsy Christmas
Just in Case You Ever Wonder
Lucado Treasury of Bedtime Prayers
One Hand, Two Hands
Thank You, God, for Blessing Me
Thank You, God, for Loving Me
The Boy and the Ocean
The Crippled Lamb
The Oak Inside the Acorn
The Tallest of Smalls
You Are Mine
You Are Special

YOUNG ADULT BOOKS

3:16
It's Not About Me
Make Every Day Count
Wild Grace
You Were Made to Make a Difference

GIFT BOOKS

Fear Not Promise Book
For the Tough Times
God Thinks You're Wonderful
Grace for the Moment
Grace Happens Here
Happy Today
His Name Is Jesus
Let the Journey Begin
Live Loved
Mocha with Max
Safe in the Shepherd's Arms
This Is Love
You Changed My Life

anxious

for

nothing

FINDING CALM *in a* CHAOTIC WORLD

MAX LUCADO

THOMAS NELSON
Since 1798

Published in Nashville, Tennessee, by Thomas Nelson. Thomas Nelson is a registered trademark of HarperCollins Christian Publishing, Inc.

Thomas Nelson titles may be purchased in bulk for educational, business, fund-raising, or sales promotional use. For information, please e-mail SpecialMarkets@ThomasNelson.com.

Any Internet addresses, phone numbers, or company or product information printed in this book are offered as a resource and are not intended in any way to be or to imply an endorsement by Thomas Nelson, nor does Thomas Nelson vouch for the existence, content, or services of these sites, phone numbers, companies, or products beyond the life of this book.

Unless otherwise noted, Scripture quotations are taken from the New King James Version®. © 1982 by Thomas Nelson. Used by permission. All rights reserved.

Scripture quotations marked AMPC are from the Amplified® Bible, Classic Edition, copyright © 1954, 1958, 1962, 1964, 1965, 1987 by The Lockman Foundation. Used by permission. (www.Lockman.org). Scripture quotations marked ESV are from the ESV® Bible (The Holy Bible, English Standard Version®), copyright © 2001 by Crossway, a publishing ministry of Good News Publishers. Used by permission. All rights reserved. Scripture quotations marked HCSB are from the Holman Christian Standard Bible®, copyright © 1999, 2000, 2002, 2003, 2009 by Holman Bible Publishers. Used by permission. HCSB® is a federally registered trademark of Holman Bible Publishers. Scripture quotations marked ISV are from the International Standard Version. Copyright © 1995–2014 by ISV Foundation. All rights reserved internationally. Used by permission of Davidson Press, LLC. Scripture quotations marked KJV are from the King James Version. Scripture quotations marked THE MESSAGE are from *The Message*. Copyright © by Eugene H. Peterson 1993, 1994, 1995, 1996, 2000, 2001, 2002. Used by permission of Tyndale House Publishers, Inc. Scripture quotations marked NASB are from the New American Standard Bible®. Copyright © 1960, 1962, 1963, 1968, 1971, 1972, 1973, 1975, 1977, 1995 by The Lockman Foundation. Used by permission. (www.Lockman.org). Scripture quotations marked NCV are from the New Century Version®. © 2005 by Thomas Nelson. Used by permission. All rights reserved. Scripture quotations marked NIV are from the Holy Bible, New International Version®, NIV®. Copyright © 1973, 1978, 1984, 2011 by Biblica, Inc.™ Used by permission of Zondervan. All rights reserved worldwide. www.zondervan.com. The "NIV" and "New International Version" are trademarks registered in the United States Patent and Trademark Office by Biblica, Inc.™ Scripture quotations marked NLT are from the *Holy Bible*, New Living Translation. © 1996, 2004, 2007, 2013, 2015 by Tyndale House Foundation. Used by permission of Tyndale House Publishers, Inc., Carol Stream, Illinois 60188. All rights reserved. Scripture quotations marked NRSV are from the New Revised Standard Version Bible. Copyright © 1989 National Council of the Churches of Christ in the United States of America. Used by permission. All rights reserved. Scripture quotations marked PHILLIPS are from J. B. Phillips: THE NEW TESTAMENT IN MODERN ENGLISH, Revised Edition. © J. B. Phillips 1958, 1960, 1972. Used by permission of Macmillan Publishing Co., Inc. Scripture quotations marked RSV are from the Revised Standard Version of the Bible, copyright 1946, 1952, and 1971 National Council of the Churches of Christ in the United States of America. Used by permission. All rights reserved. Scripture quotations marked TLB are from The Living Bible. Copyright © 1971. Used by permission of Tyndale House Publishers, Inc., Carol Stream, Illinois 60188. All rights reserved. Scripture quotations marked THE VOICE are from *The Voice*™. © 2012 by Ecclesia Bible Society. Used by permission. All rights reserved. Note: Italics in quotations from The Voice are used to "indicate words not directly tied to the dynamic translation of the original language" but that "bring out the nuance of the original, assist in completing ideas, and . . . provide readers with information that would have been obvious to the original audience" (The Voice, preface).

All hymns are taken from the public domain unless otherwise noted.

ISBN: 978-0-7180-9612-0 (HC)
ISBN: 978-0-7180-9894-0 (IE)
ISBN: 978-0-7180-7421-0 (TP)

Library of Congress Control Number: 2017933165

PRINTED IN ITALY

21   GV   16

———— ◆ ————

*It is with great joy that Denalyn and I dedicate
this book to Kahu Billy and Jenny Mitchell and the
wonderful congregation of Mana Christian Ohana.
For fifteen years you have made your home our home
away from home. We hold you dearly in our hearts.*

CONTENTS

SECTION 3: LEAVE YOUR CONCERNS WITH HIM
With thanksgiving . . .

SECTION 4: MEDITATE ON GOOD THINGS
Think about things that are worthy of praise.

ACKNOWLEDGMENTS

The team behind this book has no peer. They know their craft. They are devoted to their mission, and most of all they put up with this author. Many of these friends have worked with me for more than thirty years. I'm even more grateful to them today than I was when we began.

Editors Liz Heaney and Karen Hill. You coax, cajole, applaud, and approve. Each paragraph bears your adept touch. Thank you.

Copy editor Carol Bartley. You are to a manuscript what a skilled gardener is to a garden. No weeds permitted.

Steve and Cheryl Green. And so God said, "Let Max have two angels as escorts." And he sent Steve and Cheryl.

The Thomas Nelson superteam of Mark Schoenwald, David Moberg, LeeEric Fesko, Janene MacIvor, Jessalyn Foggy, and Laura Minchew. I'm honored to work with you.

Research assistant Sara Jones. Thanks for reading the volumes of books. And thanks, most of all, for being my daughter.

———◆———

Brand team managers Greg and Susan Ligon. No one I know has more energy, savvy, diplomacy, and skill. I'm grateful.

Administrative assistants Janie Padilla and Margaret Mechinus. You are the very picture of servanthood.

Our ever-growing family: Brett, Jenna, and Rosie; Andrea; Jeff and Sara. I'm pigeon chested with pride at the thought of you.

And Denalyn, my dear wife. Every day is made sweeter by your presence. Every person is made better by your words. And every time I look at you, I look at heaven and whisper, "Thank you, Lord."

Chapter 1

LESS FRET,
MORE FAITH

It's a low-grade fear. An edginess, a dread. A cold wind that won't stop howling.

It's not so much a storm as the certainty that one is coming. Always . . . coming. Sunny days are just an interlude. You can't relax. Can't let your guard down. All peace is temporary, short-term.

It's not the sight of a grizzly but the suspicion of one or two or ten. Behind every tree. Beyond every turn. Inevitable. It's just a matter of time until the grizzly leaps out of the shadows, bares its fangs, and gobbles you up, along with your family, your friends, your bank account, your pets, and your country.

There's trouble out there! So you don't sleep well.

You don't laugh often.
You don't enjoy the sun.
You don't whistle as you walk.

And when others do, you give them a look. *That* look. That "are you naive" look. You may even give them a word. "Haven't you read the news and heard the reports and seen the studies?"

Airplanes fall out of the sky. Bull markets go bear. Terrorists terrorize. Good people turn bad. The other shoe will drop. Fine print will be found. Misfortune lurks out there; it's just a matter of time.

Anxiety is a meteor shower of what-ifs. What if I don't close the

———•———

3

sale? What if we don't get the bonus? What if we can't afford braces for the kids? What if my kids have crooked teeth? What if crooked teeth keep them from having friends, a career, or a spouse? What if they end up homeless and hungry, holding a cardboard sign that reads "My parents couldn't afford braces for me"?

Anxiety is a meteor shower of what-ifs.

Anxiety is trepidation.

It's a suspicion, an apprehension. Life in a minor key with major concerns. Perpetually on the pirate ship's plank.

You're part Chicken Little and part Eeyore. The sky is falling, and it's falling disproportionately on you.

As a result you are anxious. A free-floating sense of dread hovers over you, a caul across the heart, a nebulous hunch about things . . . that might happen . . . sometime in the future.

Anxiety and fear are cousins but not twins. Fear sees a threat. Anxiety imagines one.

Fear screams, *Get out!*

Anxiety ponders, *What if?*

Fear results in fight or flight. Anxiety creates doom and gloom. Fear is the pulse that pounds when you see a coiled rattlesnake in your front yard. Anxiety is the voice that tells you, *Never, ever, for the rest of your life, walk barefooted through the grass. There might be a snake . . . somewhere.*

The word *anxious* defines itself. It is a hybrid of *angst* and *xious*. *Angst* is a sense of unease. *Xious* is the sound I make on the tenth step of a flight of stairs when my heart beats fast and I run low on oxygen. I can be heard inhaling and exhaling, sounding like the second syllable of *anxious*, which makes me wonder if anxious people

---

aren't just that: people who are out of breath because of the angst of life.

A native Hawaiian once told me the origin of the name that islanders use for us non-Hawaiians—*haole*. *Haole* is a Hawaiian word for "no breath." The name became associated with the European immigrants of the 1820s.[1] While there are varying explanations for this term, I like the one he gave me: "Our forefathers thought the settlers were always in a hurry to build plantations, harbors, and ranches. To the native Hawaiians they seemed short of breath."

Anxiety takes our breath, for sure. If only that were all it took. It also takes our sleep. Our energy. Our well-being. "Do not fret," wrote the psalmist, "it only causes harm" (Ps. 37:8). Harm to our necks, jaws, backs, and bowels. Anxiety can twist us into emotional pretzels. It can make our eyes twitch, blood pressure rise, heads ache, and armpits sweat. To see the consequences of anxiety, just read about half the ailments in a medical textbook.

Anxiety and fear are cousins but not twins. Fear sees a threat. Anxiety imagines one.

Anxiety ain't fun.

Chances are that you or someone you know seriously struggles with anxiety. According to the National Institute of Mental Health, anxiety disorders are reaching epidemic proportions. In a given year nearly fifty million Americans will feel the effects of a panic attack, phobias, or other anxiety disorders. Our chests will tighten. We'll feel dizzy and light-headed. We'll fear crowds and avoid people. Anxiety disorders in the United States are the "number one mental health problem among . . . women and are second only to alcohol and drug abuse among men."[2]

———•———

"The United States is now the most anxious nation in the world."[3] (Congratulations to us!) The land of the Stars and Stripes has become the country of stress and strife. This is a costly achievement. "Stress-related ailments cost the nation $300 billion every year in medical bills and lost productivity, while our usage of sedative drugs keeps sky-rocketing; just between 1997 and 2004, Americans more than doubled their spending on anti-anxiety medications like Xanax and Valium, from $900 million to $2.1 billion."[4] The *Journal of the American Medical Association* cited a study that indicates an exponential increase in depression. People of each generation in the twentieth century "were three times more likely to experience depression" than people of the preceding generation.[5]

How can this be? Our cars are safer than ever. We regulate food and water and electricity. Though gangs still prowl our streets, most Americans do not live under the danger of imminent attack. Yet if worry were an Olympic event, we'd win the gold medal!

Citizens in other countries ironically enjoy more tranquility. They experience one-fifth the anxiety levels of Americans, despite having fewer of the basic life necessities. "What's more, when these less-anxious developing-world citizens immigrate to the United States, they tend to get just as anxious as Americans. Something about our particular way of life, then, is making us less calm and composed."[6]

Our college kids are feeling it as well. In a study that involved more than two hundred thousand incoming freshmen, "students reported all-time lows in overall mental health and emotional stability."[7] As psychologist Robert Leahy points out, "The average *child* today exhibits the same level of anxiety as the average *psychiatric patient* in the 1950s."[8] Kids have more toys, clothes, and opportunities than ever, but by the time they leave home, they are wrapped tighter than Egyptian mummies.

———•———

We are tense.

Why? What is the cause of our anxiety?

Change, for one thing. Researchers speculate that the Western world's "environment and social order have changed more in the last thirty years than they have in the previous three hundred"![9] Think what has changed. Technology. The existence of the Internet. Increased warnings about global warming, nuclear war, and terrorist attacks. Changes and new threats are imported into our lives every few seconds thanks to smartphones, TVs, and computer screens. In our grandparents' generation news of an earthquake in Nepal would reach around the world some days later. In our parents' day the nightly news communicated the catastrophe. Now it is a matter of minutes. We've barely processed one crisis, and then we hear of another.

In addition we move faster than ever before. Our ancestors traveled as far as a horse or camel could take them during daylight. But us? We jet through time zones as if they were neighborhood streets. Our great-grandparents had to turn down the brain sensors when the sun set. But us? We turn on the cable news, open the laptop, or tune in to the latest survival show. For years I kept a nightly appointment with the ten o'clock news. Nothing like falling to sleep with the accounts of murders and catastrophes fresh on the brain.

And what about the onslaught of personal challenges? You or someone you know is facing foreclosure, fighting cancer, slugging through a divorce, or battling addiction. You or someone you know is bankrupt, broke, or going out of business.

Without exception we are getting older. And with age comes a covey of changes. My wife found an app that guesses a person's age by evaluating a picture of the person's face. It missed Denalyn's age by fifteen years to the young side. She liked that. It missed mine by five years to the old side. So I retook it. It added seven more. Then ten. I quit before it pronounced me dead.

One would think Christians would be exempt from worry. But we are not. We have been taught that the Christian life is a life of peace, and when we don't have peace, we assume the problem lies within us. Not only do we feel anxious, but we also feel guilty about our anxiety! The result is a downward spiral of worry, guilt, worry, guilt.

It's enough to cause a person to get anxious.

It's enough to make us wonder if the apostle Paul was out of touch with reality when he wrote, "Be anxious for nothing" (Phil. 4:6).

"Be anxious for less" would have been a sufficient challenge. Or "Be anxious only on Thursdays." Or "Be anxious only in seasons of severe affliction."

But Paul doesn't seem to offer any leeway here. Be anxious for nothing. Nada. Zilch. Zero. Is this what he meant? Not exactly. He wrote the phrase in the present active tense, which implies an ongoing state. It's the life of *perpetual anxiety* that Paul wanted to address. The *Lucado Revised Translation* reads, "Don't let anything in life leave you perpetually breathless and in angst." The presence of anxiety is unavoidable, but the prison of anxiety is optional.

> *The presence of anxiety is unavoidable, but the prison of anxiety is optional.*

Anxiety is not a sin; it is an emotion. (So don't be anxious about feeling anxious.) Anxiety can, however, lead to sinful behavior. When we numb our fears with six-packs or food binges, when we spew anger like Krakatau, when we peddle our fears to anyone who will buy them, we are sinning. If toxic anxiety leads you to abandon your spouse, neglect your kids, break covenants, or break hearts, take heed. Jesus gave this word: "Be careful, or your hearts will be weighed down with . . . the anxieties of life" (Luke 21:34 NIV). Is your heart weighed down with worry?

Look for these signals:

- Are you laughing less than you once did?
- Do you see problems in every promise?
- Would those who know you best describe you as increasingly negative and critical?
- Do you assume that something bad is going to happen?
- Do you dilute and downplay good news with doses of your version of reality?
- Many days would you rather stay in bed than get up?
- Do you magnify the negative and dismiss the positive?
- Given the chance, would you avoid any interaction with humanity for the rest of your life?

If you answered yes to most of these questions, I have a friend for you to meet. Actually, I have a scripture for you to read. I've read the words so often that we have become friends. I'd like to nominate this passage for the Scripture Hall of Fame. The museum wall that contains the framed words of the Twenty-third Psalm, the Lord's Prayer, and John 3:16 should also display Philippians 4:4–8.

Rejoice in the Lord always. Again I will say, rejoice! Let your gentleness be known to all men. The Lord is at hand. Be anxious for nothing, but in everything by prayer and supplication, with thanksgiving, let your requests be made known to God; and the peace of

God, which surpasses all understanding, will guard your hearts and minds through Christ Jesus. Finally, brethren, whatever things are true, whatever things are noble, whatever things are just, whatever things are pure, whatever things are lovely, whatever things are of good report, if there is any virtue and if there is anything praiseworthy—meditate on these things.

Five verses with four admonitions that lead to one wonderful promise: "the peace of God, which surpasses all understanding, will guard your hearts and minds" (v. 7).

Celebrate God's goodness. "Rejoice in the Lord always" (v. 4).
Ask God for help. "Let your requests be made known to God"
    (v. 6).
Leave your concerns with him. "With thanksgiving . . ." (v. 6).
Meditate on good things. "Think about the things that are good
    and worthy of praise" (v. 8 NCV).

Celebrate. Ask. Leave. Meditate. C.A.L.M.

Could you use some calm? If so, you aren't alone. The Bible is Kindle's most highlighted book. And Philippians 4:6–7 is the most highlighted passage.[10] Apparently we all could use a word of comfort. God is ready to give it.

With God as your helper, you will sleep better tonight and smile more tomorrow. You'll reframe the way you face your fears. You'll learn how to talk yourself off the ledge, view bad news through the lens of sovereignty, discern the lies of Satan, and tell yourself the truth. You will discover a life that is characterized by calm and will develop tools for facing the onslaughts of anxiety.

It will require some work on your part. I certainly don't mean to leave the impression that anxiety can be waved away with a simple pep talk. In fact, for some of you God's healing will include the help of therapy and/or medication. If that is the case, do not for a moment think that you are a second-class citizen of heaven. Ask God to lead you to a qualified counselor or physician who will provide the treatment you need.

Anxiety is not a sin; it is an emotion. (So don't be anxious about feeling anxious.)

This much is sure: It is not God's will that you lead a life of perpetual anxiety. It is not his will that you face every day with dread and trepidation. He made you for more than a life of breath-stealing angst and mind-splitting worry. He has a new chapter for your life. And he is ready to write it.

I have a childhood memory that I cherish. My father loved corn bread and buttermilk. (Can you guess that I was raised in a small West Texas town?) About ten o'clock each night he would meander into the kitchen and crumble a piece of corn bread into a glass of buttermilk. He would stand at the counter in his T-shirt and boxer shorts and drink it.

He then made the rounds to the front and back doors, checking the locks. Once everything was secure, he would step into the bedroom I shared with my brother and say something like, "Everything is secure, boys. You can go to sleep now."

I have no inclination to believe that God loves corn bread and buttermilk, but I do believe he loves his children. He oversees your world. He monitors your life. He doesn't need to check the doors; indeed, he is the door. Nothing will come your way apart from his permission.

———•———

It is not God's will that you lead a life of perpetual anxiety. It is not his will that you face every day with dread and trepidation. He made you for more than a life of breath-stealing angst and mind-splitting worry. He has a new chapter for your life. And he is ready to write it.

Listen carefully and you will hear him say, "Everything is secure. You can rest now." By his power you will "be anxious for nothing" and discover the "peace . . . which passes all understanding" (RSV).

Dear Lord,

You spoke to storms. Would you speak to ours? You calmed the hearts of the apostles. Would you calm the chaos within us? You told them to fear not. Say the same to us. We are weary from our worry, battered and belittled by the gales of life. Oh Prince of Peace, bequeath to us a spirit of calm.

As we turn the page in this book, will you turn a new leaf in our lives? Quench anxiety. Stir courage. Let us know less fret and more faith.

In Jesus' name, amen.

Section 1

—◆—

CELEBRATE GOD'S GOODNESS

Rejoice in the Lord always.

Chapter 2

REJOICE IN THE LORD'S SOVEREIGNTY

*You can't run the world, but you
can entrust it to God.*

———•———

I grew up in a camping family. My dad's idea of a great vacation involved mountains, creeks, tents, and sleeping bags. Let others tour the big cities or enjoy the theme parks. The Lucado family passed on Mickey and headed for the Rockies.

I attempted to continue this tradition with my own family. No luck. Our idea of roughing it is staying at the in-laws. We like campfires . . . as long as someone else builds them and room service is available. I'm not as hardy as my dad.

He loved camping gear as much as he loved camping trips. One day when I was about nine years old, he returned from a trip to the army surplus store with a tent that became a part of Lucado family lore.

It was huge. It could hold a dozen cots. We could erect the tent around a picnic table and still have room for sleeping bags. A big tent, of course, requires stable tent poles. This one came with two. Don't confuse these poles with the slender, retractable, aluminum versions that come with the average-size camping tent. No sirree, Bob. These poles were made of cast iron and were as thick as a forearm. The shelter wasn't fancy. No zippered doors. No mosquito netting. No camouflage design. But it was sturdy. Let the winds howl. Let the summer rains fall. Let the hail pound. Let the weather change. We weren't going anywhere.

On one occasion we were camped at Estes Park, Colorado, along with Dad's eight siblings. The sky suddenly grew dark and stormy.

Rain popped the ground, and wind bent the pine trees. Everyone made a dash for their tents. Within moments everyone left their tents and scampered to ours. It was, after all, the one with two cast-iron poles.

I'm thinking you and I could use a set of those poles. The world has a way of brewing some fierce winds. Who among us hasn't sought protection from the elements of life?

If only our storms were limited to wind and rain. Our tempests consist of the big Ds of life: difficulties, divorce, disease, and death. Does anybody know where to find a shelter that is suitable for these gales?

The apostle Paul did. If anyone had reason to be anxious, it was he. Let your imagination transport you two thousand years back in time. Envision an old man as he gazes out the window of a Roman prison.

Paul is about sixty years old, thirty years a Christian, and there is scarcely a seaport on the Mediterranean he doesn't know.

See how stooped he is? All angles and curves. Blame his bent back on the miles traveled and the beatings endured. He received thirty-nine lashes on five different occasions. He was beaten with rods on three. Scars spiderweb across his skin like bulging veins. He was once left for dead. He has been imprisoned, deserted by friends and coworkers, and has endured shipwrecks, storms, and starvation.

He's probably half-blind, squinting just to read (Gal. 4:15). What's more, he is awaiting trial before the Roman emperor. Nero has learned to curry the favor of the Roman citizens by killing believers, of which Paul is the best known.

As if the oppression from the empire weren't enough, Paul also bears the weight of newborn churches. The members are bickering. False preachers are preaching out of pride and envy (Phil. 1:15–17).

So much for the easy life of an apostle.

———◦———

His future is as gloomy as his jail cell.

Yet to read his words, you'd think he'd just arrived at a Jamaican beach hotel. His letter to the Philippians bears not one word of fear or complaint. Not one! He never shakes a fist at God; instead, he lifts his thanks to God and calls on his readers to do the same.

"Rejoice in the Lord always. Again I will say, rejoice!" (Phil. 4:4). Paul's prescription for anxiety begins with a call to rejoice.

Paul used every tool in the box on this verse, hoping to get our attention. First, he employed a present imperative tense so his readers would hear him say, continually, habitually rejoice![1] And if the verb tense wasn't enough, he removed the

> *Paul's prescription for anxiety begins with a call to rejoice.*

expiration date. "Rejoice in the Lord *always*" (emphasis mine). And if perchance the verb tense and *always* were inadequate, he repeated the command: *"Again I will say, rejoice!"* (emphasis mine).

But how can a person obey this command? Rejoice always? Is it possible for any person to maintain an uninterrupted spirit of gladness? No. This is not Paul's challenge. We are urged to "Rejoice *in the Lord.*" This verse is a call, not to a feeling, but to a decision and a deeply rooted confidence that God exists, that he is in control, and that he is good.

The apostle held firm to this belief. He had erected cast-iron stabilizers in the center of his soul. Let Nero rage. Let preachers self-promote. Let storms blow. Paul's tent of faith would never collapse. He had stabilized it with a sturdy belief system.

How sturdy is yours?

Flip back the flaps of your soul, and you'll see a series of beliefs that serve like poles to stabilize your life. Your belief system is your answer to the fundamental questions about life: Is anyone in control of the universe? Does life have a purpose? Do I have value? Is this life all there is?

Your belief system has nothing to do with your skin color, appearance, talents, or age. Your belief system is not concerned with the exterior of the tent but the interior. It is the set of convictions (poles)—all of them unseen—upon which your faith depends. If your belief system is strong, you will stand. If it is weak, the storm will prevail.

Belief always precedes behavior.

Belief always precedes behavior. For this reason the apostle Paul in each of his epistles addressed convictions before he addressed actions. To change the way a person responds to life, change what a person believes about life. The most important thing about you is your belief system.

Paul's was Gibraltar strong.

Take a close look at the poles in the tent of the apostle, and you will see one with this inscription: the sovereignty of God. *Sovereignty* is the term the Bible uses to describe God's perfect control and management of the universe. He preserves and governs every element. He is continually involved with all created things, directing them to act in a way that fulfills his divine purpose.

In the treatment of anxiety, a proper understanding of sovereignty is huge. Anxiety is often the consequence of perceived chaos. If we sense we are victims of unseen, turbulent, random forces, we are troubled.

Psychologists verified this fact when they studied the impact of combat on soldiers in World War II. They determined that after sixty days of continuous combat the ground troops became "emotionally

Free will?

dead." This reaction is understandable. Soldiers endured a constant threat of bomb blitzes, machine guns, and enemy snipers. The anxiety of ground troops was no surprise.

The comparative calm of fighter pilots, however, was. Their mortality rate was among the highest in combat. Fifty percent of them were killed in action, yet dogfighters loved their work. An astounding 93 percent of them claimed to be happy in their assignments even though the odds of survival were the same as the toss of a coin.[2]

What made the difference? Those pilots had their hands on the throttle. They sat in the cockpit. They felt that their fate was theirs to determine.[3] Infantrymen, by contrast, could just as easily be killed standing still or running away. They felt forlorn and helpless. The formula is simple: Perceived control creates calm. Lack of control gives birth to fear.

You don't need a war to prove this formula. Road congestion will do just fine. A team of German researchers found that a traffic jam increases your chances of a heart attack threefold.[4] Makes sense. Gridlock is the ultimate loss of control. We may know how to drive, but that fellow in the next lane doesn't! We can be the best drivers in history, but the texting teenager might be the end of us. There is no predictability, just stress. Anxiety increases as perceived control diminishes.

So what do we do?

Control everything? Never board a plane without a parachute. Never enter a restaurant without bringing your own clean silverware. Never leave the house without a gas mask. Never give away your heart for fear of a broken one. Never step on a crack lest you break your mother's back. Face anxiety by taking control.

Anxiety increases as perceived control diminishes.

———•———

If only we could.

Yet certainty is a cruel impostor. A person can accumulate millions of dollars and still lose it in a recession. A health fanatic can eat only nuts and veggies and still battle cancer. A hermit can avoid all human contact and still struggle with insomnia. We want certainty, but the only certainty is the lack thereof.

That's why the most stressed-out people are control freaks. They fail at the quest they most pursue. The more they try to control the world, the more they realize they cannot. Life becomes a cycle of anxiety, failure; anxiety, failure; anxiety, failure. We can't take control, because control is not ours to take.

The Bible has a better idea. Rather than seeking total control, relinquish it. You can't run the world, but you can entrust it to God. This is the message behind Paul's admonition to "rejoice *in the Lord*." Peace is within reach, not for lack of problems, but because of the presence of a sovereign Lord. Rather than rehearse the chaos of the world, rejoice in the Lord's sovereignty, as Paul did. "The things which happened to me have actually turned out for the furtherance of the gospel, so that it has become evident to the whole palace guard, and to all the rest, that my chains are in Christ" (Phil. 1:12–13).

> *Rather than rehearse the chaos of the world, rejoice in the Lord's sovereignty, as Paul did.*

And those troublemakers in the church? Those who preached out of "envy and strife" (Phil. 1:15)? Their selfish motives were no match for the sovereignty of Jesus. "Whether their motives are false or genuine, the message about Christ is being preached either way, so I rejoice. And I will continue to rejoice" (Phil. 1:18 NLT).

Paul believed that "God highly exalted [Jesus] and gave Him the name that is above every name" (Phil. 2:9 HCSB).

Conditions might have been miserable in the prison, but high above it all was a "God who works in you both to will and to do for His good pleasure" (Phil. 2:13).

To read Paul is to read the words of a man who, in the innermost part of his being, believed in the steady hand of a good God. He was protected by God's strength, preserved by God's love. He lived beneath the shadow of God's wings.

Do you?

Stabilize your soul with the sovereignty of God. He reigns supreme over every detail of the universe. "There is no wisdom, no insight, no plan that can succeed against the LORD" (Prov. 21:30 NIV). "[God] does as he pleases with the powers of heaven and the peoples of the earth. No one can hold back his hand or say to him: 'What have you done?'" (Dan. 4:35 NIV). He "sustains all things" (Heb. 1:3 NRSV). He can "whistle for the fly that is in the farthest part of the rivers of Egypt" (Isa. 7:18). He names the stars and knows the sparrows. Great and small, from the People's Liberation Army of China to the army ants in my backyard, everything is under his control. "Who can act against you without the Lord's permission? It is the Lord who helps one and harms another" (Lam. 3:37–38 TLB).

God's answer for troubled times has always been the same: heaven has an occupied throne. This was certainly the message God gave to the prophet Isaiah. During the eighth century BC, ancient Judah enjoyed a time of relative peace, thanks to the steady leadership of Uzziah, the king. Uzziah was far from perfect, yet he kept the enemies at bay. Though antagonists threatened from all sides, the presence of Uzziah kept the fragile society safe from attack for fifty-two years.

Then Uzziah died. Isaiah, who lived during the reign of the king, was left with ample reason for worry. What would happen to the people of Judah now that Uzziah was gone?

Or, in your case, what will happen now that your job is gone? Or your health has diminished? Or the economy has taken a nosedive? Does God have a message for his people when calamity strikes?

He certainly had a word for Isaiah. The prophet wrote:

In the year that King Uzziah died, I saw the Lord sitting on a throne, high and lifted up, and the train of His robe filled the temple. Above it stood seraphim; each one had six wings: with two he covered his face, with two he covered his feet, and with two he flew. And one cried to another and said:

"Holy, holy, holy, is the LORD of hosts;
The whole earth is full of His glory!" (Isa. 6:1–3)

Uzziah's throne was empty, but God's was occupied. Uzziah's reign had ended, but God's had not. Uzziah's voice was silent, but God's was strong (Isa. 6:8–10). He was, and is, alive, on the throne, and worthy of endless worship.

God calmed the fears of Isaiah, not by removing the problem, but by revealing his divine power and presence.

Think of it this way. Suppose your dad is the world's foremost orthopedic surgeon. People travel from distant countries for him to treat them. Regularly he exchanges damaged joints for healthy ones. With the same confidence that a mechanic changes spark plugs, your dad removes and replaces hips, knees, and shoulders.

At ten years of age you are a bit young to comprehend the accomplishments of a renowned surgeon. But you're not too young

Stabilize your soul with

the sovereignty of God. He

reigns supreme over every

detail of the universe.

to stumble down the stairs and twist your ankle. You roll and writhe on the floor and scream for help. You are weeks away from your first school dance. This is no time for crutches. No time for limping. You need a healthy ankle! Yours is anything but.

Into the room walks your dad, still wearing his surgical scrubs. He removes your shoe, peels back your sock, and examines the injury. You groan at the sight of the tennis ball–sized bump. Adolescent anxiety kicks in.

"Dad, I'll never walk again!"

"Yes, you will."

"No one can help me!"

"I can."

"No one knows what to do!"

"I do."

"No, you don't!"

Your dad lifts his head and asks you a question. "Do you know what I do for a living?"

Actually you don't. You know he goes to the hospital every day. You know that people call him "doctor." Your mom thinks he is smart. But you don't really know what your father does.

"So," he says as he places a bag of ice on your ankle, "it's time for you to learn." The next day he is waiting for you in the school parking lot after classes. "Hop in. I want you to see what I do," he says. He drives you to his hospital office and shows you the constellation of diplomas on his wall. Adjacent to them is a collection of awards that include words like *distinguished* and *honorable*. He hands you a manual of orthopedic surgery that bears his name.

"You wrote this?"

"I did."

His cell phone rings. After the call he announces, "We're off to surgery." You scrub up and follow him into the operating room on your crutches. During the next few minutes you have a ringside seat for a procedure in which he reconstructs an ankle. He is the commandant of the operating room. He never hesitates or seeks advice. He just does it.

One of the nurses whispers, "Your dad is the best."

As the two of you ride home that evening, you look at your father. You see him in a different light. If he can conduct orthopedic surgery, he can likely treat a swollen ankle. So you ask, "You think I'll be okay for the dance?"

"Yes, you'll be fine."

This time you believe him. Your anxiety decreases as your understanding of your father increases.

Here is what I think: our biggest fears are sprained ankles to God.

Here is what else I think: a lot of people live with unnecessary anxiety over temporary limps.

Your anxiety decreases as your understanding of your father increases.

The next time you fear the future, rejoice in the Lord's sovereignty. Rejoice in what he has accomplished. Rejoice that he is able to do what you cannot do. Fill your mind with thoughts of God.

"[He is] the Creator, who is blessed forever" (Rom. 1:25).

"[He] is the same yesterday, today, and forever" (Heb. 13:8).

"[His] years will never end" (Ps. 102:27 NIV).

———•———

He is king, supreme ruler, absolute monarch, and overlord of all history.

An arch of his eyebrow and a million angels will pivot and salute. Every throne is a footstool to his. Every crown is papier-mâché next to his. He consults no advisers. He needs no congress. He reports to no one. He is in charge.

Sovereignty gives the saint the inside track to peace. Others see the problems of the world and wring their hands. We see the problems of the world and bend our knees.

Jeremiah did.

> My soul has been rejected from peace;
> I have forgotten happiness.
> So I say, "My strength has perished,
> And so has my hope from the LORD."
> Remember my affliction and my wandering, the wormwood
> and bitterness.
> Surely my soul remembers
> And is bowed down within me. (Lam. 3:17–20 NASB)

Jeremiah was the prophet to Judah during one of her darkest periods of rebellion. They called him the weeping prophet because he was one. He wept at the condition of the people and the depravity of their faith. He was anxious enough to write a book called Lamentations. But then he considered the work of God. He purposefully lifted his mind to thoughts about his king. Note the intentionality in his words:

> This I recall to my mind,
> Therefore I have hope.

———— • ————

Others see the problems of the

world and wring their hands.

We see the problems of the

world and bend our knees.

———— • ————

The LORD's lovingkindnesses indeed never cease,
For His compassions never fail.
They are new every morning;
Great is Your faithfulness.
"The LORD is my portion," says my soul,
"Therefore I have hope in Him."
The LORD is good to those who wait for Him,
To the person who seeks Him.
It is good that he waits silently
For the salvation of the LORD. (Lam. 3:21–26 NASB)

Lift up your eyes. Don't get lost in your troubles. Dare to believe that good things will happen. Dare to believe that God was speaking to you when he said, "In everything God works for the good of those who love him" (Rom. 8:28 NCV). The mind cannot at the same time be full of God and full of fear. "He will keep in perfect peace all those who trust in him, whose thoughts turn often to the Lord!" (Isa. 26:3 TLB). Are you troubled, restless, sleepless? Then rejoice in the Lord's sovereignty. I dare you—I double-dog dare you—to expose your worries to an hour of worship. Your concerns will melt like ice on a July sidewalk.

The mind cannot at the same time be full of God and full of fear.

Anxiety passes as trust increases. In another Scripture, Jeremiah draws a direct connection between faith and peace.

Blessed is the man who trusts in the LORD,
And whose hope is the LORD.

For he shall be like a tree planted by the waters,
Which spreads out its roots by the river,
And will not fear when heat comes;
But its leaf will be green,
And *will not be anxious* in the year of drought. (Jer. 17:7–8,
    emphasis mine)

Many years ago I spent a week visiting the interior of Brazil with a longtime missionary pilot. He flew a circuit of remote towns in a four-seat plane that threatened to come undone at the slightest gust of wind. Wilbur and Orville had a sturdier aircraft.

I could not get comfortable. I kept thinking the plane was going to crash in some Brazilian jungle and I'd be gobbled up by piranhas or swallowed by an anaconda. I kept shifting around, looking down, and gripping my seat. (As if that would help.) Finally the pilot had enough of my squirming. He looked over at me and shouted over the airplane noise, "We won't face anything that I can't handle. You might as well trust me to fly the plane."

Is God saying the same to you?

Examine the poles that sustain your belief. Make sure one of them is etched with the words "My God is sovereign."

Chapter 3

REJOICE IN THE LORD'S MERCY

Guilt frenzies the soul. Grace calms it.

M y hangover was terrible, but I could survive the headache. The nausea was palpable, but I knew it would pass.

The discipline was severe, but I deserved it.

What I couldn't bear was the guilt.

I was taught from a young age that drunkenness is wrong. Our family tree is marked by a blight of alcoholism. My dad made it clear: alcohol abuse leads to trouble, and that trouble leads to misery. He regularly took me to rehab centers to visit his siblings for their benefit and ours. The battle of the bottle cost them their marriages, jobs, and health. He urged me to learn from their mistakes. More than once I promised I would never get drunk.

Then why did I? Why did my friend and I, at the age of sixteen, get so ragingly inebriated that neither of us could drive safely? Why did I drive anyway? Why did I drink so much that I went to bed with head a-spinning and stomach a-turning? Why did I get so commode-hugging drunk that I could not stand?

Did I honestly think my dad wouldn't hear me throw up? (He did.) Did I think he would believe my excuse about Mexican food? (He didn't.) When I awoke the next morning, I had a pounding head, an angry father, and this: a guilty conscience.

There is a guilt that sits in the soul like a concrete block and causes a person to feel bad for being alive. There is a guilt that says, *I did bad.* And then there is a guilt that concludes, *I am bad.* It was this deep, dark guilt that I felt. I found myself face-to-face with a version of me I had never known.

Maybe there is someone on the planet who has not known this quagmire of remorse, but I've never met that person. What sucked you under? A one-night stand? Back-street brawls? Did you pocket what wasn't yours? Or maybe your guilt is the result not of a moment in life but of a season of life. You failed as a parent. You blew it in your career. You squandered your youth or your money.

The result? Guilt.

A harsh consequence of the guilt? Anxiety.

Surprised? Lists of anxiety triggers typically include busy schedules, unrealistic demands, or heavy traffic. But we must go deeper. Behind the frantic expressions on the faces of humanity is unresolved regret.

Behind the frantic expressions on the faces of humanity is unresolved regret.

Indeed, humanity's first occasion of anxiety can be attributed to guilt. "That evening [Adam and Eve] heard the sound of the Lord God walking in the garden; and they hid themselves among the trees" (Gen. 3:8 TLB).

What had happened to the first family? Until this point there was no indication they felt any fear or trepidation. They had never hidden from God. Indeed, they had nothing to hide. "The man and his wife were both naked, but they felt no shame" (Gen. 2:25 NLT).

But then came the serpent and the forbidden fruit. The first couple said yes to the serpent's temptation and no to God. And when they did, their world collapsed like an accordion. They scurried into the bushes and went into hiding, feeling a mélange of shame and dread. Bearing crumbs from the cookie jar they were told to avoid, they engaged in a flurry of cover-ups.

Note the sequence. Guilt came first. Anxiety came in tow. Guilt drove the truck, but anxiety bounced in the flatbed. Adam and Eve didn't know how to process their failure. Neither do we. But still we try. We don't duck into the bushes. We have more sophisticated ways to deal with our guilt. We . . .

Numb it. With a bottle of Grey Goose. With an hour of Internet pornography. With a joint of marijuana, a rendezvous at the motel. Guilt disappears during happy hour, right? Funny how it reappears when we get home.

Deny it. Pretend we never stumbled. Concoct a plan to cover up the bad choice. One lie leads to another, then another. We adjust the second story to align with the first. Before long our knee-jerk reaction to any question is, how can I prolong the charade?

Minimize it. We didn't sin; we just lost our way. We didn't sin; we got caught up in the moment. We didn't sin; we just took the wrong path. We experienced a lapse in judgment.

Bury it. Suppress the guilt beneath a mound of work and a calendar of appointments. The busier we stay, the less time we spend with the people we have come to dislike most: ourselves.

Punish it. Cut ourselves. Hurt ourselves. Beat up ourselves. Flog ourselves. If not with whips, then with rules. More rules. Long lists of things to do and observances to keep. Painful penance. Pray more! Study more! Give more! Show up earlier; stay up later.

Avoid the mention of it. Just don't bring it up. Don't tell the family, the preacher, the buddies. Keep everything on the surface, and hope the Loch Ness monster of guilt lingers in the deep.

———•———

Redirect it. Lash out at the kids. Take it out on the spouse. Yell at the employees or the driver in the next lane.

Offset it. Determine never to make another mistake. Build the perfect family. Create the perfect career. Score perfect grades. Be the perfect Christian. Everything must be perfect: hair, car, tone of voice. Stay in control. Be absolutely intolerant of slipups or foul-ups by self or others.

Embody it. We didn't get drunk; we are drunks. We didn't screw up; we are screwups. We didn't just do bad; we are bad. Bad to the bone. We might even take pride in our badness. It's only a matter of time until we do something bad again.

Adam and Eve hid behind fig leaves, bushes, and lies. Not much has changed.

Let's go back to the story of sixteen-year-old Max and envision the teenager who woke up in a prodigal's pigpen. Suppose he decides to treat his shame with one of the above options or a combination thereof. Perhaps he downplays or dismisses the event. Maybe he opts for the road of pitiless self-punishment. Then again, he could anesthetize the regret with more liquor.

What will happen to Max if he never discovers a healthy treatment for failure? What kind of person does unresolved guilt create? An anxious one, forever hiding, running, denying, pretending. As one man admitted, "I was always living a lie for fear someone might see me for who I really was and think less of me, disapprove of me, reject or judge me. So I hid behind my fig leaf of competence or knowledge or superspirituality or a whole list of other options. Living this lie was exhausting and anxiety producing."[1]

Unresolved guilt will turn you into a miserable, weary, angry, stressed-out, fretful mess. In a psalm David probably wrote after his affair with Bathsheba, the king said:

—•—

When I refused to confess my sin,

my body wasted away,

and I groaned all day long.

Day and night your hand of discipline was heavy on me.

My strength evaporated like water in the summer heat.

(Ps. 32:3–4 NLT)

Guilt sucks the life out of our souls.

Grace restores it.

The apostle Paul clung to this grace. To the same degree that he believed in God's sovereignty, he relied on God's mercy.

No one had more reason to feel the burden of guilt than Paul did. He had orchestrated the deaths of Christians. He was an ancient version of a terrorist, taking believers into custody and then spilling their blood. "Paul was like a wild man, going everywhere to devastate the believers, even entering private homes and dragging out men and women alike and jailing them" (Acts 8:3 TLB).

Guilt sucks the life out of our souls. Grace restores it.

In addition, he was a legalist to the core. Before he knew Christ, Paul had spent a lifetime trying to save himself. His salvation depended on his perfection, on his performance.

If anyone ever had reason to hope that he could save himself, it would be I. If others could be saved by what they are, certainly I could! For I went through the Jewish initiation ceremony when I was eight days old, having been born into a pure-blooded Jewish home that was a branch of the old original Benjamin family. So I was a real Jew if there ever was one! What's more, I was a member of the Pharisees who demand the strictest obedience to every Jewish law and custom. And sincere? Yes, so much so that I greatly persecuted the Church; and I tried to obey every Jewish rule and regulation right down to the very last point. (Phil. 3:4–6 TLB)

Paul had blood on his hands and religious diplomas on his wall.

But then came the Damascus road moment. Jesus appeared. Once Paul saw Jesus, he couldn't see anymore. He couldn't see value in his résumé anymore. He couldn't see merit in his merits or worth in his good works anymore. He couldn't see reasons to boast about anything he had done anymore. And he couldn't see any option except to spend the rest of his life talking less about himself and more about Jesus.

He became the great poet of grace. "But all these things that I once thought very worthwhile—now I've thrown them all away so that I can put my trust and hope in Christ alone" (Phil. 3:7 TLB).

In exchange for self-salvation, God gave Paul righteousness. "Now I am right with God, not because I followed the law, but because I believed in Christ" (Phil. 3:9 NCV).

Paul gave his guilt to Jesus. Period. He didn't numb it, hide it, deny it, offset it, or punish it. He simply surrendered it to Jesus. As a result, he would write, "I am still not all I should be, but I am bringing all my energies to bear on this one thing: Forgetting the past and looking forward to what lies ahead, I strain to reach the end of the race and receive the prize for which God is calling us up to heaven because of what Christ Jesus did for us" (Phil. 3:13–14 TLB).

What would the apostle say to a guilt-laden teenager? Simply this: "Rejoice in the Lord's mercy. Trust in his ability to forgive. Abandon any attempt at self-salvation or justification. No more hiding behind fig leaves. Cast yourself upon the grace of Christ and Christ alone."

A happy saint is one who is at the same time aware of the severity of sin and the immensity of grace. Sin is not diminished, nor is God's ability to forgive it. The saint dwells in grace, not guilt. This is the tranquil soul.

God's grace is the fertile soil out of which courage sprouts. As Paul told Titus, "God's readiness to give and forgive is now public. Salvation's available for everyone! . . . Tell them all this. Build up their courage" (Titus 2:11, 15 THE MESSAGE).

I can bear witness to the power of this grace. I could take you to the city, to the church within the city, to the section of seats within the church auditorium. I might be able to find the very seat in which I was sitting when this grace found me. I was a twenty-year-old college sophomore. For four years I had lived with the concrete block of guilt, not just from that first night of drunkenness but also a hundred more like it. The guilt had made a mess of my life, and I was headed toward a lifetime of misery. But then I heard a preacher do for me what I'm attempting to do for you: describe the divine grace that is greater than sin. When at the end of the message he asked if anyone would like to come forward and receive this grace, iron chains could not have held me back. Truth be told, chains had held me back. But mercy snapped the guilt chains and set me free. I know this truth firsthand: guilt frenzies the soul; grace calms it.

That was forty years ago. In the intervening years various breeds of anxiety have stalked me. But guilt-based anxiety? No sir. The benefit of being a great sinner is dependence upon a great grace. I found a forgiveness that is too deep to be plumbed, too high to be summited. I have never been more or less saved than the moment I was first saved.

A happy saint is one who is at the same time aware of the severity of sin and the immensity of grace. Sin is not diminished, nor is God's ability to forgive it.

Not one bad deed has deducted from my salvation. No good deed, if there are any, has enhanced it. My salvation has nothing to do with my work and everything to do with the finished work of Christ on the cross.

Do you know this grace? If not, we have stumbled upon a source of your anxiety. You thought the problem was your calendar, your marriage, your job. In reality it is this unresolved guilt.

> *My salvation has nothing to do with my work and everything to do with the finished work of Christ on the cross.*

Don't indulge it. Don't drown in the bilge of your own condemnation. There is a reason the windshield is bigger than the rearview mirror. Your future matters more than your past. God's grace is greater than your sin. What you did was not good. But your God *is* good. And he will forgive you. He is ready to write a new chapter in your life. Say with Paul, "Forgetting the past and looking forward to what lies ahead, I strain to reach the end of the race and receive the prize for which God is calling us" (Phil. 3:13–14 TLB).

Denalyn and I enjoyed a nice dinner at a local restaurant the other night. About the same time we received our bill, we received a visit from a church member. He spotted us and came over to say hello. After we chatted for a moment, he reached down and took our bill and said, "I'll take this." (What a godly man.)

When he took it, guess what I did. I let him! I even ordered extra dessert. (Not really.) I just let him do what he wanted to do: I let him take it away.

Someday we will all stand before God. All of us will be present. All of us will have to give an account for our lives. Every thought, every deed, every action. Were it not for the grace of Christ, I would find this to be a terrifying thought.

Yet, according to Scripture, Jesus came to "take away the sins of the world" (John 1:29 PHILLIPS). On the day when I appear before the judgment seat of God, I will point to Christ. When my list of sins is produced, I will gesture toward him and say, "He took it."

Let him take yours.

In the great trapeze act of salvation, God is the catcher, and we are the flyers. We trust. Period.

In one of Henri Nouwen's books, he tells about the lesson of trust he learned from a family of trapeze artists known as the Flying Rodleighs. He visited with them for a time after watching them fly through the air with elegant poise. When he asked one of the flyers the secret of trapeze artists, the acrobat gave this reply:

> The secret is that the flyer does nothing and the catcher does everything. When I fly to Joe [my catcher], I have simply to stretch out my arms and hands and wait for him to catch me and pull me safely over the apron. . . .
>
> The worst thing the flyer can do is to try to catch the catcher. I am not supposed to catch Joe. It's Joe's task to catch me. If I grabbed Joe's wrists, I might break them, or he might break mine, and that would be the end for both of us. A flyer must fly, and a catcher must catch, and the flyer must trust, with outstretched arms, that his catcher will be there for him.[2]

There is a reason the windshield

is bigger than the rearview

mirror. Your future matters

more than your past.

In the great trapeze act of salvation, God is the catcher, and we are the flyers. We trust. Period. We rely solely upon God's ability to catch us. As we do, a wonderful thing happens: we fly.

Your Father has never dropped anyone. He will not drop you. His grip is sturdy and his hands are open. As the apostle proclaimed, "And *I know* the Lord will continue to rescue me from every *trip, trap, snare, and pitfall of* evil and carry me safely to His heavenly kingdom. May He be glorified throughout eternity. Amen" (2 Tim. 4:18 THE VOICE).

Place yourself entirely in his care. As you do, you will find it is possible—yes, possible!—to be anxious for nothing.

Chapter 4

REJOICE IN THE LORD *ALWAYS*

God uses everything to accomplish his will.

Place a finger on each of your temples. Now offer this prayer: *Thank you, Lord, for my amygdalae. Thank you, Lord, for the two almond-shaped neural clusters that reside inside my brain. I wouldn't be alive without them.*

The truth is, you wouldn't. Thanks to your amygdalae, you ran for cover when the grizzly growled, you stepped back on the curb when the car honked, and you ducked your head when the baseball screamed in your direction.

Your amygdalae operate like an alarm system. If an intruder breaks a window or pries open a lock to your house, your home security system warns you. Bells, alarms, horns, lights! Get up, get out, and get safe! The system alerts you before you have time to think about it.

Amygdalae do the same. We don't consciously think, *A car is coming. I'm in its way. The car is big; I am small. The car is fast; I am slow. I better move.* Amygdalae prompt a reaction before we know one is needed. And when the amygdalae command, the rest of the body reacts. Our pupils dilate, improving our vision. We breathe faster, pumping more oxygen into the lungs. Our pulse rate increases, infusing more blood into the system. Adrenaline turns us into Hercules. We are faster, stronger, better able to escape danger or fight through it. Surface-level blood vessels constrict, reducing trauma-related blood loss in the moments after injury. Even the bowel system reacts, sometimes embarrassingly, by jettisoning the unnecessary weight of what we had for lunch. We are ready for fight or flight, suddenly faster, stronger, and more alert.[1]

We like our amygdalae.

We don't like supersensitive ones, however. We don't want a home system that goes off at the gust of a breeze or the bark of a dog. We don't want that in our homes. Nor do we want that in our heads.

Perpetual anxiety is amygdalae with an itchy trigger finger. They see a mole on the skin and think cancer. They see a dip in the economy and think recession. They hear the teenagers complain and conclude, *They'll be on drugs before they leave the house.* Perpetual anxiety is the mental alarm system that never quite turns off.

> *Perpetual anxiety is amygdalae with an itchy trigger finger.*

Limited anxiety is helpful. We need to be alerted to danger. What we don't need is to live in a state of high alert.

Here is why. God created our brains to replenish themselves with natural mood elevators and tranquilizers like dopamine and serotonin. These restore joy and peace. But if the amygdalae never stop, the natural tranquilizers never have an opportunity to do their work. The brain never resets. We become edgy, unsettled, and restless. That is the bad news. The good news is this: God can calm our amygdalae! And he may very well use the words of the apostle Paul to do so.

Paul urges us to "rejoice in the Lord *always*" (Phil. 4:4, emphasis mine). Not just on paydays, Fridays, good days, or birthdays. But rejoice in the Lord always. You aren't the first to read the word *always* and arch an eyebrow. *Rejoice in the Lord always?*

"Yeah, right," mumbles the reader from the hospital bed.

"How?" sighs the unemployed dad.

———•———

"Always?" questions the mother of the baby born with a disability. It is one thing to rejoice in the Lord when life is good, but when the odds are against you?

Joseph knew this challenge. This Old Testament hero predated the apostle Paul by about twenty centuries. But both knew the challenge of imprisonment. Joseph's jail was dank and dark, a dungeon of underground, windowless rooms, stale food, and bitter water. He had no way out.

And he had no friend to help him. He thought he did. He had befriended two men from Pharaoh's court. One was a butler, the other a baker, and both were troubled by their dreams. Joseph had a knack for dream interpretation and offered to help. He had bad news for the baker ("Get your affairs in order; you're going to die.") and good news for the butler ("Get your bags packed; you're going back to Pharaoh."). Joseph asked the butler to put in a good word for him. The butler agreed. Joseph's heart raced; his hopes soared. He kept an eye on the jail door, expecting to be released any minute.

"The chief cupbearer [butler], however, did not remember Joseph; he forgot him" (Gen. 40:23 NIV). So had everyone else, it seemed. Joseph's story is one of abandonment.

His brothers had disliked his dreams and swagger and decided to kill him and throw him into a pit. Had their greed not been a feather heavier than their thirst for blood, he would have died. When they had a chance to sell him to traveling merchants, they did.

His father was uninvolved. You'd hope to read of the sudden appearance of Jacob, who searched for his son, rescued him, and took him home. We don't, because Jacob didn't. He was MIA.

Joseph was carted off to Egypt and raffled off like a farm animal. The great-grandson of Abraham was sold to the highest bidder.

———•———

Even so, he landed on his feet. He worked his way to the top of Potiphar's household. But then the mistress of the house put the hanky-panky on him. The lady went shady, and Joseph got out, leaving her holding his coat. When she accused him of attempted rape, her husband took her side and tossed Joseph in prison. Joseph landed in jail for a crime he didn't commit.

Still, he didn't give up. He became a model prisoner. He made his bed, made friends, and made a good impression on the warden, who recognized him as inmate of the month and promoted Joseph to convict-in-charge. Joseph met the butler and requested help. The butler agreed but quickly forgot, and cruelty tipped the scales. Joseph languished in prison for two years with no word and no solution.

Two years! Plenty of time to give up. Plenty of time for the world to turn gray, for gargoyles of dread to appear. Plenty of time to wonder, *Is this how God treats his children? Is this God's reward for good behavior? Do your best, and this is what you get? A jail cell and a hard bed.*

If Joseph asked such questions, we don't know. But if you ask those questions, you aren't alone.

Denalyn and I spent the better part of last evening listening as a wife told us of her husband's latest affair. This is dalliance number three. She thought they had worked through the infidelity. The bridge of trust was enjoying some fresh mortar and reinforcement. They were talking more. Fighting seldom. Life seemed to be on a good path.

Then she saw the charge on the credit card. She confronted him. He became defensive. She came undone. He walked out. It's a mess.

She asked between sobs, "Where is God in all this?"

And you? You weren't thrown in jail, like Joseph, but then again, maybe you were. Or you ended up in AA or a women's shelter or an unemployment line. And you wonder, *I believe in God. Is he aware? Does he care?*

Deism says no. God created the universe and then abandoned it.

Pantheism says no. Creation has no story or purpose unto itself; it is only a part of God.

Atheism says no. Not surprisingly, the philosophy that dismisses the existence of a god will, in turn, dismiss the possibility of a divine plan.

Christianity, on the other hand, says, "Yes, there is a God. Yes, this God is personally and powerfully involved in his creation."

"The Son is the radiance of God's glory and the exact representation of his being, sustaining all things by his powerful word" (Heb. 1:3 NIV). The Greek word that is translated *sustaining* is a term commonly used in the New Testament for "carrying" or "bringing."[2] The friends *carried* the paralyzed man to Jesus, and the servants *brought* wine to the master of the wedding. They "sustained" the man and the wine (Luke 5:18; John 2:8). They guaranteed the safe delivery.

To say Jesus is "sustaining all things by his powerful word" is to say he is directing creation toward a desired aim. The use of the present participle implies that Jesus is continually active in his creation. He exercises supremacy over all things.

Distant? Removed? Not God. "He is before all things, and in him all things hold together" (Col. 1:17 NIV). Were he to step back, the creation would collapse. His resignation would spell our evaporation. "For in him we live and move and have our being" (Acts 17:28 NIV).

Because of him, the water stays wet and the rocks remain firm. The laws of gravity and thermodynamics don't change from generation to generation. With his hand at the helm of creation, spring still follows winter, and winter follows autumn. There is an order to the universe. He sustains everything.

And this is crucial: he uses everything to accomplish his will. He "works out everything in conformity with the purpose of his will" (Eph. 1:11 NIV). The phrase "works out" comes from the Greek word *energeō*.[3] God is the energy and energizing force behind everything. No moment, event, or detail falls outside of his supervision. He stands before the universe like a symphony conductor before the orchestra, calling forth the elements to play their part in the divine reprise.

> He makes grass grow for the cattle,
> and plants for people to cultivate—
> bringing forth food from the earth:
> wine that gladdens human hearts,
> oil to make their faces shine,
> and bread that sustains their hearts. (Ps. 104:14–15 NIV)

God is the one who "causes his sun to rise on the evil and the good, and sends rain on the righteous and the unrighteous" (Matt. 5:45 NIV). God is the one who feeds the birds and watches the sparrows (Matt. 6:26; 10:29). God is the one in charge of everything, even the details of our lives.

He isn't making up this plan as he goes along. And he didn't wind up the clock and walk away. "The Most High God rules the kingdom of men, and sets over it whom he will" (Dan. 5:21 RSV). He "executes judgment, putting down one and lifting up another" (Ps. 75:7 NRSV). "The fierce anger of the LORD will not turn back until he has executed and accomplished the intents of his mind" (Jer. 30:24 NRSV).

Such starchy verbs: God "rules," "sets," "executes," "accomplished." These terms attest to the existence of a heavenly Architect and blueprint, and his blueprint includes you. "In him we were also chosen, . . .

---

according to the plan of him who works out everything in conformity with the purpose of his will" (Eph. 1:11 NIV).

So if God is in charge, why was Joseph in prison? Why is our friend's marriage in disarray? Why does God permit challenges to come our way? Wouldn't an almighty God prevent them?

Not if they serve his higher purpose. Remember the rest of Joseph's story? When Pharaoh was troubled by his dreams, the butler recalled Joseph's request. He mentioned Joseph to Pharaoh, and as fast as you can say *providence*, Joseph went from prison to palace. Joseph interpreted the dream, which was a forecast of a famine. Pharaoh promoted him to prime minister, and Joseph successfully navigated the crisis and saved not just the Egyptians but also the family of Jacob.

Years later Joseph would tell his brothers, "You intended to harm me, but God intended it for good to accomplish what is now being done, the saving of many lives. So then, don't be afraid. I will provide for you and your children" (Gen. 50:20–21 NIV). Two words at the heart of this passage reveal the heart of providential hope: *but God.* "You intended to harm me, but God . . ." What was intended as harm became good. Why? Because Joseph kept God in the middle of his circumstance.

Joseph viewed the sufferings of his life through the lens of divine providence. Can I urge you to do the same? If you don't, anxiety will stalk you every day of your life. Quite honestly, I have no words to counter the stress of the atheist or agnostic. What alleviates their anxiety? Yoga? Deep-breathing exercises? Stress-relief candles? Seems like going to a joust with a toothpick.

God's sovereignty, on the other hand, bids us to fight the onslaught of fret with the sword that is etched with the words *but God.*

The company is downsizing, *but God* is still sovereign.

The cancer is back, *but God* still occupies the throne.

I was a jerk during the first years of my marriage, *but God* showed me how to lead a family.

I was an anxious, troubled soul, *but God* has been giving me courage.

The brothers had every intention to harm Joseph. But God, in his providence, used their intended evil for ultimate good. He never robbed the brothers of their free will. He never imposed his nature upon them. But neither did he allow their sin and their sin nature to rule the day. He rerouted evil into good. God uses all things to bring about his purpose. He will not be deterred in his plan to sustain and carry creation to its intended glory.

> *God's sovereignty bids us to fight the onslaught of fret with the sword that is etched with the words* but God.

The ultimate proof of providence is the death of Christ on the cross. No deed was more evil. No other day was so dark. Yet God not only knew of the crucifixion; he ordained it. As Peter told the murderers, "This man was handed over to you by God's deliberate plan and foreknowledge; and you, with the help of wicked men, put him to death by nailing him to the cross. *But God* raised him from the dead, freeing him from the agony of death, because it was impossible for death to keep its hold on him" (Acts 2:23–24 NIV, emphasis mine).

Everyone thought the life of Jesus was over—*but God*. His Son was dead and buried, but God raised him from the dead. God took the crucifixion of Friday and turned it into the celebration of Sunday.

Can he not do a reversal for you?

I'm sorry for the pain that life has given you. I'm sorry if your parents neglected you. I'm sorry if your teacher ignored you. I'm sorry if a heartbreaker said "I do" on your wedding day but "I don't" every day afterward. I'm sorry if you were inappropriately touched, intentionally mocked, or unfairly dismissed. I'm sorry if you ended up in Egypt.

But if the story of Joseph teaches us anything, it is this: we have a choice. We can wear our hurt or wear our hope. We can outfit ourselves in our misfortune, or we can clothe ourselves in God's providence. We can cave in to the pandemonium of life, or we can lean into the perfect plan of God. And we can believe this promise: "In all things God works for the good of those who love him, who have been called according to his purpose" (Rom. 8:28 NIV).

In the famous lace shops of Brussels, Belgium, certain rooms are dedicated to the spinning of the finest lace with the most delicate of patterns. These rooms are completely dark, save for a shaft of natural light from a solitary window. Only one spinner sits in the room. The light falls upon the pattern while the worker remains in the dark.[4]

God took the crucifixion of Friday and turned it into the celebration of Sunday.

Has God permitted a time of darkness in your world? You look but cannot see him. You see only the fabric of circumstances woven and interlaced. You might question the purpose behind this thread or that. But be assured, God has a pattern. He has a plan. He is not finished, but when he is, the lace will be beautiful.

Some time ago I made a special visit to the American Colony Hotel in Jerusalem. I was in Israel with a long list of places to visit and sites

You might question the purpose

behind this thread or that. But be

assured, God has a pattern. He has

a plan. He is not finished, but when

he is, the lace will be beautiful.

to see. But at the top of the list was a visit to the lobby of the American Colony Hotel. I placed it on my itinerary not because I, too, am an American. Not because the food in the restaurant is tasty or the facility is particularly nice. The food is tasty and the establishment is terrific, but I went for another reason. I wanted to see the handwritten lyrics that hang on the wall, framed and visible for all to see.

Horatio Spafford wrote the lyrics, never imagining they would become the words to one of the world's best-loved hymns. Spafford was a prosperous lawyer and Presbyterian Church elder. In 1871 he and his wife, Anna, suffered tragic losses in the Chicago fire. In November of 1873, Anna and their children set sail for Europe with a group of friends. Horatio stayed home to take care of some business. On December 2 he received a telegram from his wife that began "Saved alone. What shall I do?"[5] He soon learned that the ship had collided with a British vessel and had sunk. Their four daughters drowned and Anna survived. He left for England to bring Anna back home. En route, while sailing on the ship, he wrote the lyrics to a song that would become an anthem to the providence of God.

He and Anna eventually moved to Jerusalem to form a Christian society designed to minister to the needs of all people. In time the group expanded and moved into a large house outside the city walls. The house became a hostel, then a hotel. It still stands, and it still serves as the display location for these words written by a grief-stricken man on a storm-tossed sea.

"It Is Well with My Soul"

When peace, like a river, attendeth my way,
When sorrows like sea billows roll;

———•———

Whatever my lot, Thou has taught me to say,
It is well, it is well, with my soul.

Though Satan should buffet, though trials should come,
Let this blest assurance control,
That Christ has regarded my helpless estate,
And hath shed His own blood for my soul.

My sin, oh, the bliss of this glorious thought!
My sin, not in part but the whole,
Is nailed to the cross, and I bear it no more,
Praise the Lord, praise the Lord, O my soul!

And Lord, haste the day when my faith shall be sight,
The clouds be rolled back as a scroll;
The trump shall resound, and the Lord shall descend,
Even so, it is well with my soul.

It is well, with my soul,
It is well, with my soul,
It is well, it is well, with my soul.[6]

May we so trust in the providence of God that we can say the same.
Always.

Section 2

---◆---

ASK GOD FOR HELP

Let your requests be made known to God.

Chapter 5

CONTAGIOUS CALM

Anxiety is needless because God is near.

———•———

D isaster was as close as the press of a red button. Four Russian submarines patrolled the Florida coast. US warships had dropped depth charges. The Russian captain was stressed, trigger-happy, and ready to destroy a few American cities. Each sub was armed with a nuclear warhead. Each warhead had the potential to repeat a Hiroshima-level calamity.

Had it not been for the contagious calm of a clear-thinking officer, World War III might have begun in 1962. His name was Vasili Arkhipov. He was the thirty-six-year-old chief of staff for a clandestine fleet of Russian submarines. The crew members assumed they were being sent on a training mission off the Siberian coast. They came to learn that they had been commissioned to travel five thousand miles to the southwest to set up a spearhead for a base near Havana, Cuba.

The subs went south, and so did their mission. In order to move quickly, the submarines traveled on the surface of the water, where they ran head-on into Hurricane Daisy. The fifty-foot waves left the men nauseated and the operating systems compromised.

Then came the warm waters. Soviet subs were designed for the polar waters, not the tropical Atlantic. Temperatures inside the vessels exceeded 120 degrees Fahrenheit. The crew battled the heat and claustrophobia for much of the three-week journey. By the time they were near the coast of Cuba, the men were exhausted, on edge, and anxious.

The situation worsened when the subs received cryptic instructions from Moscow to turn northward and patrol the coastline of Florida. Soon after they entered American waters, their radar picked up the signal of a dozen ships and aircraft. The Russians were being followed by the Americans. The US ships set off depth charges. The Russians assumed they were under attack.

The captain lost his cool. He summoned his staff to his command post and pounded the table with his fists. "We're going to blast them now! We will die, but we will sink them all—we will not disgrace our navy!"

The world was teetering on the edge of war. But then Vasili Arkhipov asked for a moment with his captain. The two men stepped to the side. He urged his superior to reconsider. He suggested they talk to the Americans before reacting. The captain listened. His anger cooled. He gave the order for the vessels to surface.

The Americans encircled the Russians and kept them under surveillance. What they intended to do is unclear as in a couple of days the Soviets dove, eluded the Americans, and made it back home safely.

This incredible brush with death was kept secret for decades. Arkhipov deserved a medal, yet he lived the rest of his life with no recognition. It was not until 2002 that the public learned of the barely avoided catastrophe. As the director of the National Security Archive stated, "The lesson from this [event] is that a guy named Vasili Arkhipov saved the world."[1]

Why does this story matter? You will not spend three weeks in a sweltering Russian sub. But you may spend a semester carrying a heavy class load, or you may fight the headwinds of a recession. You may spend night after night at the bedside of an afflicted child or aging parent. You may fight to keep a family together, a business afloat, a school from going under.

You will be tempted to press the button and release, not nuclear warheads, but angry outbursts, a rash of accusations, a fiery retaliation of hurtful words. Unchecked anxiety unleashes an Enola Gay of destruction. How many people have been wounded as a result of unbridled stress?

And how many disasters have been averted because one person refused to buckle under the strain? It is this composure Paul is summoning in the first of a triad of proclamations. "Let your gentleness be evident to all. The Lord is near. Do not be anxious about anything" (Phil. 4:5–6 NIV).

The Greek word translated here as *gentleness* (*epieikes*) describes a temperament that is seasoned and mature.[2] It envisions an attitude that is fitting to the occasion, levelheaded and tempered. The gentle reaction is one of steadiness, evenhandedness, fairness. It "looks humanely and reasonably at the facts of a case."[3] Its opposite would be an overreaction or a sense of panic.

This gentleness is "evident to all." Family members take note. Your friends sense a difference. Coworkers benefit from it. Others may freak out or run out, but the gentle person is sober minded and clear thinking. Contagiously calm.

The contagiously calm person is the one who reminds others, "God is in control." This is the executive who tells the company, "Let's all do our part; we'll be okay." This is the leader who sees the challenge, acknowledges it, and observes, "These are tough times, but we'll get through them."

Gentleness. Where do we quarry this gem? How can you and I

> *The contagiously calm person is the one who reminds others, "God is in control."*

keep our hands away from the trigger? How can we keep our heads when everyone else is losing theirs? We plumb the depths of the second phrase. "Let your gentleness be evident to all. The Lord is near. Do not be anxious about anything" (Phil. 4:5–6 NIV).

The Lord is near! You are not alone. You may feel alone. You may think you are alone. But there is never a moment in which you face life without help. God is near.

God repeatedly pledges his proverbial presence to his people.

To Abram, God said, "Do not be afraid. . . . I am your shield, your exceedingly great reward" (Gen. 15:1).

To Hagar, the angel announced, "Do not be afraid; God has heard" (Gen. 21:17 NIV).

When Isaac was expelled from his land by the Philistines and forced to move from place to place, God appeared to him and reminded him, "Do not be afraid, for I am with you" (Gen. 26:24 NLT).

After Moses' death God told Joshua, "Do not be afraid; do not be discouraged, for the LORD your God will be with you wherever you go" (Josh. 1:9 NIV).

God was with David, in spite of his adultery. With Jacob, in spite of his conniving. With Elijah, in spite of his lack of faith.

Then, in the ultimate declaration of communion, God called himself Immanuel, which means "God with us." He became flesh. He became sin. He defeated the grave. He is still with us. In the form of his Spirit, he comforts, teaches, and convicts.

Do not assume God is watching from a distance. Avoid the quicksand that bears the marker "God has left you!" Do not indulge this lie. If you do, your problem will be amplified by a sense of loneliness. It's one thing to face a challenge, but to face it all alone? Isolation creates a downward cycle of fret. Choose instead to be the person who clutches

Isolation creates a downward cycle
of fret. Choose instead to be the
person who clutches the presence
of God with both hands.

the presence of God with both hands. "The LORD is with me; I will not be afraid. What can mere mortals do to me?" (Ps. 118:6 NIV).

Because the Lord is near, we can be anxious for nothing. This is Paul's point. Remember, he was writing a letter. He did not use chapter and verse numbers. This system was created by scholars in the thirteenth and sixteenth centuries. The structure helps us, but it can also hinder us. The apostle intended the words of verses 5 and 6 to be read in one fell swoop. "The Lord is near; [consequently,] do not be anxious about anything." Early commentators saw this. John Chrysostom liked to phrase the verse this way: "The Lord is at hand. Have no anxiety."⁴ Theodoret of Cyrus translated the words: "The Lord is near. Have no worries."⁵

We can calmly take our concerns to God because he is as near as our next breath!

This was the reassuring lesson from the miracle of the bread and fish. In an event crafted to speak to the anxious heart, Jesus told his disciples to do the impossible: feed five thousand people.

"Jesus lifted up His eyes, and seeing a great multitude coming toward Him, He said to Philip, 'Where shall we buy bread, that these may eat?' But this He said to test him, for He Himself knew what He would do" (John 6:5–6). When John described this gathering as a "great multitude," he was serious. There were five thousand men, plus women and children (Matt. 14:21). Imagine a capacity crowd at a sports arena, and you've got the picture. Jesus was willing to feed the entire crowd.

The disciples, on the other hand, wanted to get rid of everyone. "Send the multitudes away, that they may go into the villages and buy themselves food" (Matt. 14:15). I detect some anxiety in their words. I sense a tone of aggravation, frustration. They don't call Jesus "Master." They don't come to him with a suggestion. They march as a group to Christ and tell him what to do. The disciples see a valley full of hungry people. Growling stomachs will soon become scowling faces, and the disciples might have a riot on their hands. They had every reason to feel unsettled.

Then again, did they not have equal reason to feel at peace? By this point in their experience with Jesus, they had seen him

- heal leprosy (Matt. 8:3),
- heal the centurion's servant without going to the servant's bedside (Matt. 8:13),
- heal Peter's mother-in-law (Matt. 8:15),
- calm a violent sea (Matt. 8:26),
- heal a paralytic (Matt. 9:6–7),
- heal a woman who had been sick for twelve years (Matt. 9:22),
- raise a girl from the dead (Matt. 9:25),
- drive out an evil spirit (Mark 1:25),
- heal a demon-possessed man in a cemetery (Mark 5:15),
- change water into wine (John 2:9), and
- heal a man who had been an invalid for thirty-eight years (John 5:9).

Did any of the disciples pause long enough to think, *Well, hmmm. Jesus healed the sick people, raised the dead girl, and calmed the angry waves. I wonder, might he have a solution we have not seen? After all, he is standing right here. Let's ask him.*

Did it occur to anyone to ask Jesus for help?

The stunning answer is no! They acted as if Jesus weren't even present. Rather than count on Christ, they had the audacity to tell the Creator of the world that nothing could be done because there wasn't enough money.

How did Jesus maintain his composure? How did he keep from looking at the disciples and saying, "Have you forgotten who I am?"

Finally a boy offered his lunch basket to Andrew, who tentatively mentioned the offer to Jesus.

Jesus said, "Have the people sit down." There was plenty of grass in that place, and they sat down (about five thousand men were there). Jesus then took the loaves, gave thanks, and distributed to those who were seated as much as they wanted. He did the same with the fish.

When they had all had enough to eat, he said to his disciples, "Gather the pieces that are left over. Let nothing be wasted." So they gathered them and filled twelve baskets with the pieces of the five barley loaves left over by those who had eaten. (John 6:10–13 NIV)

Not one coin was spent. They started the day with two hundred coins. They ended the day with two hundred coins. In addition, they filled twelve baskets with leftover food. A souvenir for each apostle, perhaps? The people were fed, the bank account was untouched, and we have a lesson to learn: anxiety is needless, because Jesus is near.

You aren't facing five thousand hungry bellies, but you are facing a deadline in two days . . . a loved one in need of a cure . . . a child who is being bullied at school . . . a spouse intertwined in temptation. On one hand you have a problem. On the other you have a limited quantity of wisdom, energy, patience, or time. What you have is nowhere near what you need. You have a thimbleful, and you need bucketloads. Typically you'd get anxious. You'd tell God to send the problem packing. "You've given me too much to handle, Jesus!"

This time, instead of starting with what you have, start with Jesus. Start with his wealth, his resources, and his strength. Before you open the ledger, open your heart. Before you count coins or count heads, count the number of times Jesus has helped you face the impossible. Before you lash out in fear, look up in faith. Take a moment. Turn to your Father for help.

In his fine book *The Dance of Hope*, Bill Frey remembers the day he tried to pull a stump out of the Georgia dirt. He was eleven years old at the time. One of his

> *Before you lash out in fear, look up in faith.*

chores was the gathering of firewood for the small stove and fireplace of the homestead. He would search the woods for stumps of pine trees that had been cut down and chop them into kindling. The best stumps were saturated with resin and therefore would burn more easily.

> One day I found a large stump in an open field near the house and tried to unearth it. I literally pushed and pulled and crowbarred for hours, but the root system was so deep and large I simply couldn't pull it out of the ground. I was still struggling when my father came home from his office, spotted me working and came over to watch.
>
> "I think I see your problem," he said.
>
> "What's that?" I asked.
>
> "You're not using all your strength," he replied.
>
> I exploded and told him how hard I had worked and for how long.
>
> "No," he said, "you're not using all your strength."
>
> When I cooled down I asked him what he meant, and he said, "You haven't asked me to help you yet."[6]

This business of anxiety management is like pulling stumps out of the ground. Some of your worries have deep root systems. Extracting them is hard, hard work. In fact, it may be the toughest challenge of all. But you don't have to do it alone.

Present the challenge to your Father and ask for help.

Will he solve the issue? Yes, he will.

Will he solve it immediately? Maybe. Or maybe part of the test is an advanced course in patience.

This much is sure: contagious calm will happen to the degree that we turn to him.

Chapter 6

PRAYER, NOT DESPAIR

Peace happens when people pray.

---•---

The judge owned a gated mansion in the Hamptons. His swimming pool was shaped like a dollar sign. He smoked Cuban cigars, wore Armani suits, and drove a 911 Porsche Carrera coupe with a personalized license plate that bore the words *My Way*. He was on the payroll of every Mafia boss and drug dealer on the eastern seaboard. They kept him in office; he kept them out of jail. They gave him votes; he gave them a free walk.

Sweet.

He was a crook. His mother knew it. His priest knew it. His kids knew it. God knew it. The judge couldn't care less. He never gave God a second thought or an honest person a second chance. According to Jesus the judge was a scoundrel.

He certainly didn't care about the widow. "In that same town there was a widow who kept coming to this judge, saying, 'Give me my rights against my enemy'" (Luke 18:3 NCV).

We'll call her Ethel. She had a homely look to her: hair tied in a bun, plaid dress, old jogging shoes that appeared to have been rescued from a yard sale. If the judge was a Cadillac, Ethel was a clunker. But for an old clunker she had a lot of horsepower. She was determined to escape a certain adversary. A bill collector? Angry landlord? Oppressive neighbor? Someone had turned against her. Someone had resolved to take her to the cleaners. She pleaded her case and begged for justice.

No luck. She exhausted every possible solution. Finally, on a burst of chutzpah, she sought the assistance of the judge.

Every morning when he stepped out of his limo, there Ethel stood on the courthouse sidewalk. "Can I have a minute, Your Honor?"

When he exited his chambers, Ethel was waiting in the hallway. "Judge, I need your help."

At Giovanni's, where the judge ate lunch, she approached his table. "Just a few minutes of your time." How she got past the maître d', the judge never knew. But there she was.

Ethel even sat in the front row of the courtroom during trials, holding up a cardboard sign that read "Can you help me?"

During his Saturday-morning golf game, she walked out of the bushes near the fourth green. "Your Honor, I have a request."

She tapped him on the shoulder as he walked into the theater. "Pardon me, sir. I need your help."

Ethel also annoyed the judge's wife. She hounded the judge's secretary. "Do something about Ethel," they demanded. "She's a pest!"

"For a while the judge refused to help her" (v. 4 NCV).

One day when they said the coast was clear, he dashed from his office to his limo and jumped in the backseat, only to be confronted by you-know-who. Ethel was in the car! He was stuck.

He took one look at her and sighed. "Lady, you don't get it, do you? I don't like people. I don't believe in God. There is nothing good in me. Yet you keep asking me to help you."

"Just a small favor," Ethel asked, holding her thumb a quarter inch from her forefinger.

He growled through clenched teeth, "Anything to be rid of you. What do you want?"

She spilled out a story that included the words *widow*, *broke*, and the phrase *eviction notice*. The judge stared out the car window as she pleaded for his intervention. "He thought to himself, 'Even though I don't respect God or care about people, I will see that she gets her rights. Otherwise she will continue to bother me until I am worn out'" (vv. 4–5 NCV).

When she finally paused to take a breath, he waved her silent. "Okay, okay. I'll give you a break."

"You will?"

"Yes, on one condition."

"Anything."

"You get out of my life!"

"Yes, I promise." Ethel beamed. "Can I give you a hug?"

He told her no, but she did anyway.

She jumped out of the car and danced a jig on the sidewalk. The dishonest judge rode away, grumbling. And we, the readers, look up from Luke's gospel and wonder, *What is this story doing in the Bible?*

A corrupt official. A persistent gadfly. Reluctant benevolence. No compassion or concern. Is there a message in this account? Is God a reluctant judge? Are we the marginalized widow? Is prayer a matter of pestering God until he breaks down and gives us what we want?

No, this is a parable of contrast, not comparison. The judge groused, complained, murmured. Yet "even he rendered a just decision in the end. So don't you think God will surely give justice to his chosen people who cry out to him day and night? . . . I tell you, he will grant justice to them quickly!" (vv. 7–8 NLT). God is not the reluctant judge in this story. And you are not the widow. The widow in the story was at the bottom of the pecking order. She had nowhere to turn. But as a child of the King, you are at the front of the line. You, at any moment, can turn to God.

God doesn't delay. He never places you on hold or tells you to call again later. God loves the sound of your voice. Always. He doesn't hide when you call. He hears your prayers.

For that reason "be anxious for nothing, but in everything by prayer and supplication, with thanksgiving, let your requests be made known to God" (Phil. 4:6).

God loves the sound of your voice. Always.

With this verse the apostle calls us to take action against anxiety. Until this point he has been assuring us of God's character: his sovereignty, mercy, and presence. Now it is our turn to act on this belief. We choose prayer over despair. Peace happens when people pray.

I like the story of the father who was teaching his three-year-old daughter the Lord's Prayer. She would repeat the lines after him. Finally she decided to go solo. He listened with pride as she carefully enunciated each word, right up to the end of the prayer. "Lead us not into temptation," she prayed, "but deliver us from e-mail."

These days that seems like an appropriate request. God calls us to pray about everything. The terms *prayer, supplication,* and *requests* are similar but not identical. Prayer is a general devotion; the word includes worship and adoration. Supplication suggests humility. We are the supplicants in the sense that we make no demands; we simply offer humble requests. A request is exactly that—a specific petition. We tell God exactly what we want. We pray the particulars of our problems.

What Jesus said to the blind man, he says to us: "What do you want me to do for you?" (Luke 18:41 NIV). One would think the answer would be obvious. When a sightless man requests Jesus' help, isn't it apparent what he needs? Yet Jesus wanted to hear the man articulate his specific requests.

He wants the same from us. "Let your requests be made known to God." When the wedding ran low on wine, Mary wasn't content to say, "Help us, Jesus." She was specific: "They have no more wine" (John 2:3 NIV). The needy man in Jesus' parable requested, "Friend, lend me three loaves" (Luke 11:5 NIV). Not just "Give me something to eat"

> *Peace happens when people pray.*

or "Can you help me out?" He made a specific request. Even Jesus in the Garden of Gethsemane prayed specifically, "Take this cup from me" (Luke 22:42 NIV). Why does this matter? I can think of three reasons.

1. *A specific prayer is a serious prayer.* If I say to you, "Do you mind if I come by your house sometime?" you may not take me seriously. But suppose I say, "Can I come over this Friday night? I have a problem at work, and I really need your advice. I can be there at seven, and I promise I will leave by eight." Then you know my petition is sincere. When we offer specific requests, God knows the same.

2. *Specific prayer is an opportunity for us to see God at work.* When we see him respond in specific ways to specific requests, our faith grows. The book of Genesis relates the wonderful prayer of Abraham's servant. He was sent to Mesopotamia, Abraham's homeland, to find a wife for Abraham's son. How does a servant select a wife for someone else? This servant prayed about it.

> "O LORD, God of my master, Abraham," he prayed. "Please give me success today, and show unfailing love to my master,

Abraham. See, I am standing here beside this spring, and the young women of the town are coming out to draw water. This is my request. I will ask one of them, 'Please give me a drink from your jug.' If she says, 'Yes, have a drink, and I will water your camels, too!'—let her be the one you have selected as Isaac's wife. This is how I will know that you have shown unfailing love to my master." (Gen. 24:12–14 NLT)

Could the servant have been more detailed? He asked for success in his endeavor. He envisioned an exact dialogue, and then he stepped forth in faith. Scripture says, "Before he had finished speaking, Rebekah appeared" (v. 15 ISV). She said the words. The servant had an answered prayer. He saw God at work.

3. *Specific prayer creates a lighter load.* Many of our anxieties are threatening because they are ill defined and vague. If we can distill the challenge into a phrase, we bring it down to size. It is one thing to pray, *Lord, please bless my meeting tomorrow.* It is another thing to pray, *Lord, I have a conference with my supervisor at 2:00 p.m. tomorrow. She intimidates me. Would you please grant me a spirit of peace so I can sleep well tonight? Grant me wisdom so I can enter the meeting prepared. And would you soften her heart toward me and give her a generous spirit? Help us have a gracious conversation in which both of us benefit and your name is honored.* There. You have reduced the problem into a prayer-sized challenge.

This is no endorsement of the demanding, conditional prayer that presumes to tell God what to do and when. Nor do I suggest that the power of prayer resides in chanting the right formula or quoting some secret code. Do not think for a moment that the power of prayer resides in the way we present it. God is not manipulated or impressed by our formulas or eloquence. But he is moved by the sincere request. After all, is he not our Father? As his children we honor him when we tell him exactly what we need.

On my good days I begin my morning with a cup of coffee and a conversation with God. I look ahead into the day and make my requests. *I am meeting with so-and-so at 10:00 a.m. Would you give me wisdom? This afternoon I need to finish my sermon. Would you please go ahead of me?* Then if a sense of stress surfaces during the day, I remind myself, *Oh, I gave this challenge to God earlier today. He has already taken responsibility for the situation. I can be grateful, not fretful.*

"Cast all your anxiety on him because he cares for you" (1 Peter 5:7 NIV). Casting is an intentional act to relocate an object. When the disciples prepared Jesus to ride into Jerusalem on Palm Sunday, they "cast their garments upon the colt" (Luke 19:35 KJV). The crowd removed the garments off their backs and spread them in the path of Christ. Let this "throwing" be your first response to bad news. As you sense anxiety welling up inside you, cast it in the direction of Christ. Do so specifically and immediately.

I did a good job of "casting my problems" in a high school algebra class. My brain scans reveal a missing region marked by the sign "Intended for Algebra." I can remember sitting in the class and staring at the textbook as if it were a novel written in Mandarin Chinese.

Fortunately I had a wonderful, patient teacher. He issued this invitation and stuck to it. "If you cannot solve a problem, come to me and I will help you."

I wore a trail into the floor between his desk and mine. Each time I

As you sense anxiety welling

up inside you, cast it in the

direction of Christ. Do so

specifically and immediately.

had a question, I would approach his desk and remind him, "Remember how you promised you would help?" When he said yes, instant gratitude and relief kicked in. I still had the problem, mind you, but I had entrusted the problem to one who knew how to solve it.

Do the same. Take your problem to Christ and tell him, "You said you would help me. Would you?"

The Old Testament prophet Isaiah said, "Put the Lord in remembrance [of His promises], keep not silence" (Isa. 62:6 AMPC). God told Isaiah, "Put Me in remembrance; let us contend together" (Isa. 43:26). God invites you—yes, commands you—to remind him of his promises. Populate your prayer with "You said . . ."

"You said you would walk me through the waters" (Isa. 43:2, author's paraphrase).

"You said you would lead me through the valley" (Ps. 23:4, author's paraphrase).

"You said that you would never leave or forsake me" (Heb. 13:5, author's paraphrase).

Find a promise that fits your problem, and build your prayer around it. These prayers of faith touch the heart of God and activate the angels of heaven. Miracles are set into motion. Your answer may not come overnight, but it will come. And you will overcome.

"Prayer is essential in this ongoing warfare. Pray hard and long. Pray for your brothers and sisters" (Eph. 6:18 THE MESSAGE).

The path to peace is paved with prayer. Less consternation, more supplication. Fewer anxious thoughts, more prayer-filled thoughts. As you pray, the peace of God will guard your heart and mind. And, in the end, what could be better?

LEAVE YOUR CONCERNS WITH HIM

With thanksgiving . . .

Chapter 7

GREAT GRATITUDE

*Christ-based contentment turns
us into strong people.*

The widest river in the world is not the Mississippi, Amazon, or Nile. The widest river on earth is a body of water called If Only.

Throngs of people stand on its banks and cast longing eyes over the waters. They desire to cross but can't seem to find the ferry. They are convinced the If Only river separates them from the good life.

If only I were thinner, I'd have the good life.

If only I were richer, I'd have the good life.

If only the kids would come. If only the kids were gone. If only I could leave home, move home, get married, get divorced.

If only my skin were clear of pimples, my calendar free of people, my profession immune to layoffs, then I would have the good life.

The If Only river.

Are you standing on its shore? Does it seem the good life is always one *if only* away? One purchase away? One promotion away? One election, transition, or romance away?

If so, then we've traced your anxiety back to one of its sources. You're in a hurry to cross the river and worried that you never will. Consequently, you work long hours, borrow more money, take on new projects, and pile on more responsibilities. Stress. Debt. Short nights. Long days. All part of the cost of the ticket to the land of the good life, right?

Not exactly, opined the apostle Paul. The good life begins, not when circumstances change, but when our attitude toward them does.

Look again at his antidote for anxiety. "Be anxious for nothing, but in everything by prayer and supplication, with thanksgiving, let your requests be made known to God; and the peace of God, which surpasses all understanding, will guard your hearts and minds through Christ Jesus" (Phil. 4:6–7).

Paul embedded in the verses two essential words that deserve special attention: *with thanksgiving*. Sprinkled among your phrases "Help me . . . ," "Please give me . . . ," "Won't you show me . . ." should be two wonderful words: *Thank you*.

Gratitude is a mindful awareness of the benefits of life. It is the greatest of virtues. Studies have linked the emotion with a variety of positive effects. Grateful people tend to be more empathetic and forgiving of others. People who keep a gratitude journal are more likely to have a positive outlook on life. Grateful individuals demonstrate less envy, materialism, and self-centeredness. Gratitude improves self-esteem and enhances relationships, quality of sleep, and longevity.[1] If it came in pill form, gratitude would be deemed the miracle cure. It's no wonder, then, that God's anxiety therapy includes a large, delightful dollop of gratitude.

> *God's anxiety therapy includes a large, delightful dollop of gratitude.*

Gratitude leads us off the riverbank of If Only and escorts us into the fertile valley of Already. The anxious heart says, "Lord, if only I had this, that, or the other, I'd be okay." The grateful heart says, "Oh, look! You've *already* given me this, that, and the other. Thank you, God."

My friend Jerry has taught me the value of gratitude. He is seventy-eight years old and regularly shoots his age on the golf course. (If I ever do the same, I'll need to live to be a hundred.) His dear wife, Ginger, battles Parkinson's disease. What should have been a wonderful season of retirement has been marred by multiple hospital stays, medication, and struggles. Many days she cannot keep her balance. Jerry has to be at her side. Yet he never complains. He always has a smile and a joke. And he relentlessly beats me in golf. I asked Jerry his secret. He said, "Every morning Ginger and I sit together and sing a hymn. I ask her what she wants to sing. She always says, 'Count Your Blessings.' So we sing it. And we count our blessings."

Take a moment and follow Jerry's example. Look at your blessings.

Do you see any friends? Family? Do you see any grace from God? The love of God? Do you see any gifts? Abilities or talents? Skills?

As you look at your blessings, take note of what happens. Anxiety grabs his bags and slips out the back door. Worry refuses to share the heart with gratitude. One heartfelt thank-you will suck the oxygen out of worry's world. So say it often. Focus more on what you do have and less on what you don't. The apostle Paul modeled this outlook.

> I have learned to be content whatever the circumstances. I know what it is to be in need, and I know what it is to have plenty. I have learned the secret of being content in any and every situation, whether well fed or hungry, whether living in plenty or in want. I can do all this through him who gives me strength. (Phil. 4:11–13 NIV)

The circumstances of Paul's life in jail were miserable. Under constant surveillance. No reason to hope for release. Yet with shackles dangling from his wrists, the apostle announced, "I have learned the secret of being content."

Paul's use of the term *secret* is curious. He doesn't say, "I have

Worry refuses to share the heart
with gratitude. One heartfelt
thank-you will suck the oxygen
out of worry's world.

learned the *principle*." Or "I have learned the *concept*." Instead, "I have learned the *secret* of being content." A secret, by definition, is a bit of knowledge not commonly known. It is as if the apostle beckons us to lean forward to hear him whisper, "Can I share a secret about happiness?"

> I have learned the secret of being content—whether well fed or hungry, whether in abundance or in need. (v. 12 HCSB)

Does your happiness depend on what you drive? Wear? Deposit? Spray on? If so, you have entered the rat race called materialism. You cannot win it! There will always be a newer car to buy or a nicer dress to purchase. And since the race is unwinnable, you are setting yourself up for anxiety. Define yourself by stuff, and you'll feel good when you have a lot, and you'll feel bad when you don't.

The cycle is predictable. You assume, *If I get a car, I'll be happy.* You get the car, but the car wears out. You look for joy elsewhere. *If I get married, I'll be happy.* So you get married, but your spouse cannot deliver. *If we can have a baby . . . If I get the new job . . . If I can retire . . .* In each case joy comes, then diminishes. By the time you reach old age, you have ridden a roller coaster of hope and disappointment. Life has repeatedly let you down, and you are suspicious that it will let you down again.

Contingent contentment turns us into wounded, worried people.

Contingent contentment turns us into wounded, worried people.

Paul advances a healthier strategy. He learned to be content with what he had. Which is remarkable since he had so little. He had a jail cell instead of a house. He had four walls instead of the mission field. He had chains instead of jewelry, a guard instead of a wife. How could he be content?

Simple. He focused on a different list. He had eternal life. He had the love of God. He had forgiveness of sins. He had the surety of salvation. He had Christ, and Christ was enough. What he had in Christ was far greater than what he didn't have in life.

Here is an interesting detail about his letter to the Philippians. Within its 104 verses Paul mentioned Jesus forty times. At an average of every 2.5 verses, Paul was talking about Christ. "To me the only important thing about living is Christ, and dying would be profit for me" (Phil. 1:21 NCV).

> *Death, failure, betrayal, sickness, disappointment—they cannot take our joy, because they cannot take our Jesus.*

His only aim was to know Jesus. Riches did not attract him. Applause did not matter to him. The grave did not intimidate him. All he wanted was more of Christ. As a result, he was content. In Jesus, Paul found all the satisfaction his heart desired.

You and I can learn the same. Christ-based contentment turns us into strong people. Since no one can take our Christ, no one can take our joy.

Can death take our joy? No, Jesus is greater than death.

Can failure take our joy? No, Jesus is greater than our sin.

Can betrayal take our joy? No, Jesus will never leave us.

Can sickness take our joy? No, God has promised, whether on this side of the grave or the other, to heal us.

Can disappointment take our joy? No, because even though our
plans may not work out, we know God's plan will.

Death, failure, betrayal, sickness, disappointment—they cannot take
our joy, because they cannot take our Jesus.

Please underline this sentence: what you have in Christ is greater
than anything you don't have in life. You have God, who is crazy about
you, and the forces of heaven to monitor and protect you. You have the
living presence of Jesus within you. In Christ you have everything.

He can give you a happiness that can never be taken, a grace that
will never expire, and a wisdom that will ever increase. He is a fountain
of living hope that will never be exhausted.

Years ago I lived on a houseboat that was docked on the Miami
River in Miami, Florida. The level of the river would rise and fall with
the tide. It rocked back and forth with the river traffic. But though the
level changed and the boat rocked, it never drifted. Why? Because the
boat was securely anchored.

What about you?

Anchor your heart to the character of God.
Your boat will rock. Moods will come and go.
Situations will fluctuate. But will you be left
adrift on the Atlantic of despair? No, for you have
found a contentment that endures the storm.

Anchor your heart to the character of God.

No more "if only." It is the petri dish in which
anxiety thrives. Replace your "if only" with "already." Look what you
already have. Treat each anxious thought with a grateful one, and pre-
pare yourself for a new day of joy.

Chapter 8

GOD'S PEACE, YOUR PEACE

*You may be facing the perfect storm,
but Jesus offers the perfect peace.*

When mariners describe a tempest that no sailor can escape, they call it a perfect storm. Not perfect in the sense of ideal, but perfect in the sense of combining factors. All the elements, such as hurricane-force winds plus a cold front plus a downpour of rain, work together to create the insurmountable disaster. The winds alone would be a challenge; but the winds plus the cold plus the rain? The perfect recipe for disaster.

You needn't be a fisherman to experience a perfect storm. All you need is a layoff *plus* a recession. A disease *plus* a job transfer. A relationship breakup *plus* a college rejection. We can handle one challenge . . . but two or three at a time? One wave after another, gale forces followed by thunderstorms? It's enough to make you wonder, *Will I survive?*

Paul's answer to that question is profound and concise. "The peace of God, which surpasses all understanding, will guard your hearts and minds through Christ Jesus" (Phil. 4:7).

As we do our part (rejoice in the Lord, pursue a gentle spirit, pray about everything, and cling to gratitude), God does his part. He bestows upon us the peace of God. Note, this is not a peace *from* God. Our Father gives us the very peace *of* God. He downloads the tranquility of the throne room into our world, resulting in an inexplicable calm. We should be worried, but we aren't. We should be upset, but we are comforted. The peace of God transcends all logic, scheming, and efforts to explain it.

This kind of peace is not a human achievement. It is a gift from above. "Peace I leave with you; my peace I give you. I do not give to you as the world gives. Do not let your hearts be troubled and do not be afraid" (John 14:27 NIV).

Jesus promises you his vintage of peace! The peace that calmed his heart when he was falsely accused. The peace that steadied his voice when he spoke to Pilate. The peace that kept his thoughts clear and heart pure as he hung on the cross. This was his peace. This can be your peace.

The peace of God transcends all logic, scheming, and efforts to explain it.

This peace "guards [our] hearts and minds through Christ Jesus" (Phil. 4:7).

God takes responsibility for the hearts and minds of those who believe in him. As we celebrate him and pray to him, he constructs a fortress around our hearts and minds, protecting us from the attacks of the devil. As the verse from the ancient hymn declares:

A mighty fortress is our God, a bulwark never failing;
Our helper He, amid the flood of mortal ills prevailing.[1]

Martin Luther wrote these words centuries after the apostle Paul had written his epistles. Yet had Paul heard the hymn, he would have sung it with hearty conviction. He knew firsthand the peace and protection of God. In fact, he had just experienced it in the last major event of his life before his imprisonment: a sea journey from Caesarea to Rome.

When he penned the "be anxious for nothing" paragraph, he had recently endured a storm on the Mediterranean Sea. On his final recorded voyage Paul was placed on a ship in Caesarea destined for Italy. Luke traveled with him, as did Aristarchus, a Christian brother from Thessalonica. Some prisoners were on the ship, presumably condemned men who were bound for the Roman arena. The ship enjoyed smooth sailing until they reached Sidon. At the next stop, Myra, they changed vessels. They were loaded onto a large Egyptian grain ship. About one hundred feet long and weighing perhaps more than a thousand tons, the ships were sturdy but engineered in such a way that they did not sail well into the wind.[2]

They reached nearby Cnidus with great difficulty. From there they sailed south under the shelter of Crete until they reached the port of Fair Havens, about halfway across the island. Fair Havens was not "fair" on the eyes. It received this name from the chamber of commerce, I suppose, in hope of attracting business.

The sailors didn't want to stay in Fair Havens. They knew they couldn't reach Rome before winter but preferred the port of Phoenix.

Paul tried to convince them otherwise. They had reason to listen to him, because Paul was no stranger to storms at sea and shipwrecks (2 Cor. 11:25). One ancient volume described the dangers of sailing at this time of year as "scant daylight, long nights, dense cloud cover, poor visibility and the double raging of winds, showers and snows."[3] He knew the danger of a winter voyage and issued a strong caution. But in the eyes of the captain, Paul was nothing but a Jewish preacher. So they weighed anchor and set sail for a better harbor (Acts 27:1–12).

"But not long after, a tempestuous head wind arose, called Euroclydon" (v. 14). What a great word—a compound of the Greek term *euros*, the east wind, and the Latin word *aquilo*, the north wind.[4] Some translations call this wind what it was, a northeaster.[5] The temperature dropped. The sails whipped. The waves frothed. The sailors searched for land and couldn't see it. They looked at the storm and couldn't avoid it.

The components of the perfect storm were gathering:

a winter sea
a ferocious wind
a cumbersome boat
an impatient crew

Individually these elements were manageable, but collectively they were formidable. So the crew did what they could. They hoisted the lifeboat aboard and frapped the vessel. They lowered the sea anchor, jettisoned cargo, and threw equipment overboard. But nothing worked.

Verse 20 reads like a death sentence: "Now when neither sun nor stars appeared for many days, and no small tempest beat on us, all hope that we would be saved was finally given up."

The perfect storm took its toll.

It lasted for fourteen days (v. 27)! Fourteen hours would shake you. (Fourteen minutes would undo me!) But two weeks of sunless days and starless nights? Fourteen days of bouncing, climbing toward the heavens and plunging toward the sea. The ocean boomed, splashed, and rumbled. The sailors lost all appetite for food. They lost all reason for hope. They gave up. And when they gave up, Paul spoke up.

But after long abstinence from food, then Paul stood in the midst of them and said, "Men, you should have listened to me, and not have sailed from Crete and incurred this disaster and loss. And now I urge you to take heart, for there will be no loss of life among you, but only of the ship." (vv. 21–22)

———◆———

The peace that kept his thoughts

clear and heart pure as he hung

on the cross. This was his peace.

This can be your peace.

———◆———

What a contrast. The mariners, who knew how to sail in storms, gave up hope. Paul, a Jewish preacher who presumably knew very little about sailing, became the courier of courage. What did he know that they didn't?

Better question, what did he say that you need to hear? Are you bouncing about in a northeaster? Like the sailors you've done all you can to survive: you've tightened the ship, lowered the anchor. You've consulted the bank, changed your diet, called the lawyers, called your supervisor, tightened your budget. You've gone for counseling, rehab, or therapy. Yet the sea churns with angry foam. Is fear coming at you from all sides? Then let God speak to you. Let God give you what he gave the sailors: perfect peace.

Paul began with a rebuke: "Men, you should have listened to me." We don't like to be rebuked, corrected, or chastened. But when we ignore God's warnings, a scolding is in order.

> *Is fear coming at you from all sides? Then let God speak to you.*

Did you? Are you in a storm of anxiety because you didn't listen to God? He told you that sex outside of marriage would result in chaos, but you didn't listen. He told you that the borrower is a slave to the lender, but you took on the dangerous debt. He told you to cherish your spouse and nourish your kids, but you cherished your career and nourished your vices. He cautioned you about the wrong crowd and the strong drink and the long hours. But you did not listen. And now you are in a storm of your own making.

If this describes you, receive God's rebuke. He corrects those he loves, and he loves you. So stand corrected. Confess your sin and resolve to do better. Be wiser next time. Learn from your poor choice. But don't despair. While this story contains one rebuke, it also contains three promises that can give us peace in the middle of a storm.

Heaven has helpers to help you. Paul said, "There stood by me this night an angel" (v. 23). On the deck of a sinking ship in a raging storm, Paul received a visitor from heaven. An angel came and stood beside him. Angels still come and help us.

Recently after a church service one of our members approached me in the reception line. Her eyes were full of tears and wonder as she said, "I saw your angel."

"You did?"

"Yes, he stood near you as you preached."

I find comfort in that thought. I also find many scriptures to support it. "All the angels are spirits who serve God and are sent to help those who will receive salvation" (Heb. 1:14 NCV).

The prophet Daniel experienced the assistance of angels. He was troubled. He resolved to pray. After three weeks (so much for one-shot attempts at prayer), Daniel saw a man dressed in linen with a belt of gold around his waist. His body was like topaz, his face like lightning, his eyes on fire. His arms and legs resembled burnished bronze. His voice was like the roar of a multitude (Dan. 10:5–6 NIV).

Daniel was so stunned he fell to the ground. The angel said:

> "Don't be afraid, Daniel. Since the first day you began to pray for understanding and to humble yourself before your God, your request has been heard in heaven. I have come in answer to your prayer. But for twenty-one days the spirit prince of the kingdom of Persia blocked my way. Then Michael, one of the archangels, came to help me, and I left him there with the spirit prince of the kingdom

of Persia. Now I am here to explain what will happen to your people in the future." (vv. 12–14 NLT)

The moment Daniel began praying, the answer was issued. Demonic forces blocked the pathway of the angel. The impasse lasted a full three weeks until the archangel Michael arrived on the scene with his superior authority. The standoff was ended, and the prayer was answered.

Have your prayers been met with a silent sky? Have you prayed and heard nothing? Are you floundering in the land between an offered and an answered prayer? Do you feel the press of Satan's mortar and pestle?

If so, I beg you, don't give up. What the angel said to Daniel, God says to you: "Since the first day that you set your mind to gain understanding and to humble yourself before your God, your words were heard" (Dan. 10:12 NIV). You have been heard in heaven. Angelic armies have been dispatched. Reinforcements have been rallied. God promises, "I will contend with him who contends with you" (Isa. 49:25).

Do what Daniel did. Remain before the Lord.

> Those who wait on the LORD
> Shall renew their strength;
> They shall mount up with wings like eagles,
> They shall run and not be weary,
> They shall walk and not faint. (Isa. 40:31)

An angel protected Shadrach, Meshach, and Abed-Nego in the fiery furnace (Dan. 3:23–26). They can protect you. An angel escorted Peter out of prison (Acts 12:5–9). They can walk you out of your bondage. "He [God] has put his angels in charge of you to watch over you wherever you go" (Ps. 91:11 NCV). Heaven has helpers for you.

Do you believe in Angels?

And . . .

Heaven has a place for you. Paul knew this. "For there stood by me this night an angel of the God to whom I belong" (Acts 27:23).

When parents send their kids to summer camp, they have to sign certain documents. One of the documents asks, who is the responsible party? If Johnny breaks his arm or Suzie breaks out with measles, who will be responsible? Hopefully Mom and Dad are willing to sign their names.

God signed his. When you gave your life to him, he took responsibility for you. He guarantees your safe arrival into his port. You are his sheep; he is your shepherd. Jesus said, "I am the good shepherd; I know my sheep and my sheep know me" (John 10:14 NIV).

You are a bride; he is your bridegroom. The church is being "prepared as a bride adorned for her husband" (Rev. 21:2).

You are his child; he is your father. "You are no longer a slave but God's own child. And since you are his child, God has made you his heir" (Gal. 4:7 NLT).

You can have peace in the midst of the storm because you are not alone, you belong to God, and . . .

You are in the Lord's service. "For there stood by me this night an angel of the God to whom I belong and whom I serve" (Acts 27:23).

God had given Paul an assignment: carry the gospel to Rome. Paul had not yet arrived at Rome, so God was not yet finished with him. Since God was not yet finished, Paul knew he would survive.

Most of us don't have a clear message like Paul's. But we do have the assurance that we will not live one day less than we are supposed to live. If God has work for you to do, he will keep you alive to do it. "All the days planned for me were written in your book before I was one day old" (Ps. 139:16 NCV).

———•———

No life is too short or too long. You will live your prescribed number of days. You might change the quality of your days but not the quantity.

I'm not saying you will have no more problems in your future. Quite the contrary. Paul had his share, and so will you. Look at verse 22: "And now I urge you to take heart, for there will be no loss of life among you, but only of the ship" (Acts 27).

It is not easy to lose your ship. Your ship is the vessel that carries, sustains, protects, and supports you. Your boat is your marriage, your body, your business. Because of your boat, you've stayed afloat. And now without your boat you think you will sink. You're correct. You will, for a while. Waves will sweep over you. Fear will suck you under like a Pacific riptide. But take heart, says Paul. Take heart, says Christ: "In this world you will have trouble, but be brave! I have defeated the world" (John 16:33 NCV).

You can lose it all, only to discover that you haven't. God has been there all along.

God has never promised a life with no storms. But he has promised to be there when we face them. Consider the compelling testimony of Jehoshaphat. He ascended the throne at the age of thirty-five and reigned for twenty-five years.

According to the book of 2 Chronicles, the Moabites formed a great and powerful confederacy with the surrounding nations and marched against Jehoshaphat (2 Chron. 20). It was a military version of a perfect storm. The Jews could handle one army. But when one army allies with another and those two combine with a third? It was more than the king could handle.

Jehoshaphat's response deserves a spot in the anxiety-treatment textbook. He "set himself to seek the LORD" (2 Chron. 20:3). He "proclaimed a fast throughout all Judah" (v. 3). He cried out to God in prayer (vv. 6–12). He confessed, "We have no power . . . nor do we know what to do, but our eyes are upon You" (v. 12).

God responded with this message: "Do not be afraid nor dismayed because of this great multitude, for the battle is not yours, but God's" (v. 15).

Jehoshaphat so totally believed in God that he made the remarkable decision of marching into battle with singers in front. I'm confident the people who signed up for the choir never imagined they would lead the army. But Jehoshaphat knew the real battle was a spiritual one, so he led with worship and worshippers. By the time they reached the battlefield, the battle was over. The enemies had turned on each other, and the Hebrews never had to raise a sword (vv. 21–24).

Learn a lesson from the king. Lead with worship. Go first to your Father in prayer and praise. Confess to him your fears. Gather with his people. Set your face toward God. Fast. Cry out for help. Admit your weakness. Then, once God moves, you move too. Expect to see the God of ages fight for you. He is near, as near as your next breath.

Expect to see the God of ages fight for you. He is near, as near as your next breath.

Noah Drew can tell you. He was only two years old when he discovered the protective presence of Jesus.

The Drew family was making the short drive from their house to their neighborhood pool. Leigh Anna, the mom, was driving so slowly that the automatic door locks did not engage. Noah opened his door and fell out. She felt a bump, as if she had driven over a speed bump, and braked to a quick stop. Her husband,

Ben, jumped out of the car and found Noah on the pavement. "He's alive!" Ben shouted and placed him on the seat. Noah's legs were covered in blood, and he was shaking violently. Leigh Anna hurried over to the passenger's seat and held Noah on her lap as Ben drove to the ER.

Incredibly, the tests showed no broken bones. A five-thousand-pound vehicle had run over his legs, yet little Noah had nothing but cuts and bruises to show for it.

Later that night Leigh Anna dropped to her knees and thanked Jesus for sparing her son. She then stretched out on the bed next to him. He was asleep; at least she thought he was. As she was lying beside him in the dark, he said, "Mama, Jesus catched me."

She said, "He did?"

Noah replied, "I told Jesus thank you, and he said you're very welcome."

The next day he gave some details. "Mama, Jesus has brown hands. He catched me like this." He held his arms outstretched, cupping his little hands. The next day he told her that Jesus has brown hair. When she asked him for more information, he said, "That's all," in a very nonchalant manner. But when he said his prayers that night, he said, "Thank you, Jesus, for catching me."[6]

Northeasters bear down on the best of us. Contrary winds. Crashing waves. They come. But Jesus still catches his children. He still extends his arms. He still sends his angels. Because you belong to him, you can have peace in the midst of the storm. The same Jesus who sent the angel to Paul sends this message to you: "When you pass through the waters, I will be with you" (Isa. 43:2 NIV).

You may be facing the perfect storm, but Jesus offers the perfect peace.

MEDITATE ON GOOD THINGS

Think about things that are worthy of praise.

Chapter 9

THINK ABOUT WHAT YOU THINK ABOUT

*Your problem is not your problem
but the way you see it.*

———•———

In her short thirteen years Rebecca Taylor has endured more than fifty-five surgeries and medical procedures and approximately one thousand days in the hospital.

Christyn, Rebecca's mom, talks about her daughter's health complications with the ease of a surgeon. The vocabulary of most moms includes phrases such as "cafeteria food," "slumber party," and "too much time on the phone." Christyn knows this language, but she's equally fluent in the vernacular of blood cells, stents, and, most recently, a hemorrhagic stroke.

In her blog she wrote:

> This past week's new land mine was the phrase "possible hemorrhagic stroke," a phrase I heard dozens of times used by numerous physicians. Over and over and over that phrase filled my mind and consumed my thoughts. It was emotionally crippling.
>
> This past Sunday our preacher, Max Lucado, started a very fitting series on anxiety. We reviewed the familiar Philippians 4:6 verse: "Do not be anxious about anything, but in everything, by prayer and petition, with thanksgiving, present your requests to God."
>
> I presented my requests to the Lord as I had so many times before, but this time, THIS time, I needed more. And so, using Philippians 4:8–9 as a guide, I found my answer:
>
> "Finally, brothers, whatever is true . . ." What was true in my life at

this particular moment? *The blessing of all family members eating dinner together.*

"Whatever is noble." *The blessing of enjoying each other's presence outside of a hospital room.*

"Whatever is right." *The blessing of experiencing my two sons' daily lives.*

"Whatever is pure." *The blessing of all three children laughing and playing with each other.*

"Whatever is lovely." *The blessing of watching Rebecca sleep peacefully in her bed at night.*

"Whatever is admirable." *The blessing of an honorable team working tirelessly on Rebecca's care.*

"If anything is excellent." *The blessing of watching a miracle unfold.*

"Or praiseworthy." *The blessing of worshiping a Lord who is worthy to be praised.*

"Think about such things."

I did. As I meditated on these things, I stopped the dreaded phrase "hemorrhagic stroke" from sucking any joy out of my life. Its power to produce anxiety was now rendered impotent. And when I dwelt on the bountiful blessings in my life happening AT THAT VERY MOMENT, "the peace of God, which transcends all understanding," DID guard my heart and my mind in Christ Jesus. A true, unexpected miracle. Thank you, Lord.[1]

Did you note what Christyn did? The words *hemorrhagic stroke* hovered over her life like a thundercloud. Yet she stopped the dreaded phrase from sucking joy out of her life.

She did so by practicing thought management. You probably know this, but in case you don't, I am so thrilled to give you the good news: you can pick what you ponder.

You didn't select your birthplace or birth date. You didn't choose your parents or siblings. You don't determine the weather or the amount of salt in the ocean. There are many things in life over which you have no choice. But the greatest activity of life is well within your dominion. You can choose what you think about.

You can be the air traffic controller of your mental airport. You occupy the control tower and can direct the mental traffic of your world. Thoughts circle above, coming and going. If one of them lands, it is because you gave it permission. If it leaves, it is because you directed it to do so. You can select your thought pattern.

For that reason the wise man urges, "Be careful what you think, because your thoughts run your life" (Prov. 4:23 NCV). Do you want to be happy tomorrow? Then sow seeds of happiness today. (Count blessings. Memorize Bible verses. Pray. Sing hymns. Spend time with encouraging people.) Do you want to guarantee tomorrow's misery? Then wallow in a mental mud pit of self-pity or guilt or anxiety today. (Assume the worst. Beat yourself up. Rehearse your regrets. Complain to complainers.) Thoughts have consequences.

You can be the air traffic controller of your mental airport. You occupy the control tower and can direct the mental traffic of your world.

Healing from anxiety requires healthy thinking. Your challenge is not your challenge. Your challenge is the way you think about your challenge. Your problem is not your problem; it is the way you look at it.

Satan knows this. The devil is always messing with our minds. He fills the sky with airplanes that carry nothing but fear and anxiety. And he is doing his best to convince us to let them land and unload their stinking cargo into our minds. He comes as a thief "with the sole intention of stealing and killing and destroying" (John 10:10 PHILLIPS). He brings only gloom and doom. By the time he was finished with Job, the man was sick and alone. By the time he had done his work in Judas, the disciple had given up on life. The devil is to hope what termites are to an oak; he'll chew you up from the inside.

He will lead you to a sunless place and leave you there. He seeks to convince you this world has no window, no possibility of light. Exaggerated, overstated, inflated, irrational thoughts are the devil's specialty.

No one will ever love me.
It's all over for me.
Everyone is against me.
I'll never lose weight, get out of debt, or have friends.

What lugubrious, monstrous lies! No problem is unsolvable. No life is irredeemable. No one's fate is sealed. No one is unloved or unlovable. But Satan wants us to think we are. He wants to leave us in a swarm of anxious, negative thoughts.

Satan is the master of deceit. But he is not the master of your mind. You have a power he cannot defeat. You have God on your side.

So "fix your thoughts on what is true, and honorable, and right, and pure, and lovely, and admirable. Think about things that are excellent and worthy of praise" (Phil. 4:8 NLT). The transliteration of the Greek word, here rendered as *fix*, is *logizomai*. Do you see the root of an English word in the Greek one? Yes, *logic*. Paul's point is simple: anxiety is best faced with clearheaded, logical thinking.

---◆---

No problem is unsolvable.

No life is irredeemable. No

one's fate is sealed. No one

is unloved or unlovable.

---◆---

Turns out that our most valuable weapon against anxiety weighs less than three pounds and sits between our ears. Think about what you think about!

Here is how it works. You receive a call from the doctor's office. The message is simple and unwelcome. "The doctor has reviewed your tests and would like you to come into the office for a consultation."

As quickly as you can say "uh-oh," you have a choice: anxiety or trust.

Anxiety says . . .

"I'm in trouble. Why does God let bad things happen to me? Am I being punished? I must have done something wrong."

"These things never turn out right. My family has a history of tragedy. It's my turn. I probably have cancer, arthritis, jaundice. Am I going blind? My eyes have been blurry lately. Is this a brain tumor?"

"Who will raise the kids? Who will pay the medical bills? I'm going to die broke and lonely. I'm too young for this tragedy! No one can understand me or help me."

If you aren't already sick, you will be by the time you go to the doctor's office. "Anxiety weighs down the human heart" (Prov. 12:25 NRSV).

But there is a better way.

Before you call your mom, spouse, neighbor, or friend, call on God. Invite him to speak to the problem. "Capture every thought and make it give up and obey Christ" (2 Cor. 10:5 NCV). Slap handcuffs on the culprit, and march it before the One who has all authority: Jesus Christ.

Jesus, this anxious, negative thought just wormed its way into my mind. Is it from you?

Jesus, who speaks nothing but the truth, says, "No, get away from here, Satan." And as the discerning, sober-minded air traffic controller of your mind, you refuse to let the thought have the time of day.

———•———

Lay claim to every biblical promise you can remember, and set out to learn a few more. Grip them for the life preservers they are. Give Satan no quarter. Give his lies no welcome. "Fasten the belt of truth around your waist" (Eph. 6:14 NRSV). Resist the urge to exaggerate, overstate, or amplify. Focus on the facts, nothing more. The fact is, the doctor has called. The fact is, his news will be good or bad. For all you know, he may want you to be a poster child of good health. All you can do is pray and trust.

So you do. You enter the doctor's office, not heavied by worry, but buoyed by faith.

Which do you prefer?

During the very weekend I was editing this book, I put this chapter to the test. We received a call that my wife's father wasn't doing well. He had been sick for several months. He suffers from congestive heart failure and increasing dementia. He is eighty-three years old. His wife had passed into heaven a few months earlier, and he has been on a steady decline ever since.

His cardiologist told us that his heart might last only a few more weeks. He was in an assisted-living facility about five hours from our home, and Denalyn felt a strong leading that we needed to move him to our house. We drove to his city to evaluate the situation. Everything we saw confirmed what we had heard. He was weak. His thoughts were erratic. He was in need of constant care, more than the facility was equipped to provide.

Later that night in the hotel room, I told Denalyn she was right. We needed to move her father to our house.

Then came the meltdown. While the rest of the family was busy making plans, I wandered into the labyrinth of dread. I began to envision life with an elderly man in our house. The caregivers. The oxygen tank. The hospital bed. The toilet issues. The calls for help in the middle of the night.

Anxiety dragged me into a bare-knuckled MMA cage fight. By the time I went to bed, I was bruised and bloody. After a fitful night of sleep, I awoke and said to the Lord and to myself, *It is time for me to practice what I preach.* I set out to lasso in my thoughts. I began making a list of blessings. Psalm 103:2 came to mind: "O my soul, bless GOD, don't forget a single blessing" (THE MESSAGE). Rather than ponder our problems, I chose to enumerate every indication of God's presence.

For example, I needed a rental trailer. The owner of the shop turned out to be a friend of a friend.

I needed a trailer hitch. It was a Friday afternoon, and I needed it installed before Saturday. On my second call I found a shop that "just happened" to have one available and could meet the deadline.

I needed to pay the lawn worker who was caring for Denalyn's father's house. He "just happened" to be parked in front of the house when I went to check on it.

We needed to find a physician and a home-health-care team. The physician's office took my call and scheduled an appointment. The home-health-care team found a worker who could meet us at our home.

I found a buyer for the car my father-in-law had been driving.

The assisted-living facility knew someone who needed the furniture we were leaving behind.

I made the deliberate decision to interpret each of these good turns as evidence of God's blessing and presence. Little by little the gray clouds lifted, and the blue sky began to peek through. I can honestly say I sensed a peace that passes understanding.

Christyn Taylor discovered the same calmness. Recently she and her family went back to Rebecca's doctors in Minnesota. Seven months earlier Rebecca was barely surviving. Now, one day before her thirteenth birthday, Rebecca was vibrant and full of life. She had gained a remarkable thirty pounds. Her health was improving. She was named the hospital's "walking miracle."

Christyn wrote: "I watched these interactions with a silent sense of awe. It is easy to praise God during seasons of wellness. But it was during my greatest distress when I felt the Lord's presence poured upon me. And it was in those heartbreaking moments I learned to trust this God who provided unimaginable strength during unimaginable pain."[2]

Guard your thoughts and trust your Father.

He will help you as well, my friend. Guard your thoughts and trust your Father.

Chapter 10

CLING TO CHRIST

We bear fruit by focusing on God.

Farmer Jones sensed trouble on the trellis. His grape givers groaned. Leaves drooped. Vines dragged. Listless loganberries sighed in chorus.

The farmer listened for a time and decided to do what grape growers have done since the beginning of the writing of this chapter. He talked to his crop. A boss-to-branch chat was in order. He set a stool between the rows, pulled off his straw hat, took a seat, and invited, "Okay, guys. Why the gloom? This is not the *whine* I had in mind."

At first no one spoke. Finally a slender tendril opened up. "I just can't do it anymore!" he blurted. "I squeeze and push, but the grapes won't come."

Leaves bounced as other branches nodded in agreement. "I can't even get a raisin to pop out," one confessed.

"Call me cluster barren," shouted another.

"Forgive me for being sappy," offered one more, "but I'm one burdened branch. I'm so tired my bark is barking."

Farmer Jones shook his head and sighed. "No wonder you guys are unhappy. You're trying to do what you can't do and forgetting to do what you're made to do. Stop forcing the fruit. Your job is to hang on to the vine, to keep connected to the trunk. Get a grip! You'll be amazed by what you will produce."

Far-fetched conversation? Between a farmer and a vineyard, yes.

But between our Father and his children? He must hear multiple moans a minute.

"I'm a spiritual flop."

"The only fruit I bear is fear."

"Perfect peace? I feel like a perfect mess."

The phrase "fruitless and fret filled" describes too many of us. We don't want it to. We long to follow Paul's admonition: "Fix your thoughts on what is true, and honorable, and right, and pure, and lovely, and admirable. Think about things that are excellent and worthy of praise" (Phil. 4:8 NLT).

With a grimace and fresh resolve, we determine, *Today I will think only true, honorable, and right thoughts . . . even if it kills me.*

Paul's call to peace can become a list of requirements: every thought *must* be true, honorable, right, pure, lovely, admirable, excellent, and worthy of praise.

Gulp. Who can do this?

Confession: I find the list difficult to keep. Heaven knows, I've tried. A random idea will pop into my head, and I'll pass it through the passage. *Was it true, honorable, pure . . . What's next?* I have trouble remembering the eight virtues, much less remembering to filter my thoughts through them. Maybe the list works for you. If so, skip this chapter. If not, there is a simpler way.

Make it your aim to cling to Christ. Abide in him. Is he not true, honorable, right, pure, lovely, admirable, excellent, and worthy of praise? Is this not the invitation of his message in the vineyard?

Abide in Me, and I in you. As the branch cannot bear fruit of itself unless it abides in the vine, so neither can you unless you abide in Me. I am the vine, you are the branches; he who abides in Me and I in him,

Make it your aim to cling to

Christ. Abide in him. Is he not

true, honorable, right, pure,

lovely, admirable, excellent,

and worthy of praise?

he bears much fruit, for apart from Me you can do nothing. If anyone does not abide in Me, he is thrown away as a branch and dries up; and they gather them, and cast them into the fire and they are burned. If you abide in Me, and My words abide in you, ask whatever you wish, and it will be done for you. My Father is glorified by this, that you bear much fruit, and so prove to be My disciples. Just as the Father has loved Me, I have also loved you; abide in My love. If you keep My commandments, you will abide in My love; just as I have kept My Father's commandments and abide in His love. (John 15:4–10 NASB)

Jesus' allegory is simple. God is like a vine keeper. He lives and loves to coax the best out of his vines. He pampers, prunes, blesses, and cuts. His aim is singular: "What can I do to prompt produce?" God is a capable orchardist who carefully superintends the vineyard.

And Jesus plays the role of the vine. We nongardeners might confuse the vine and the branch. To see the vine, lower your gaze from the stringy, winding branches to the thick base below. The vine is the root and trunk of the plant. It cables nutrients from the soil to the branches. Jesus makes the stunning claim, "I am the real root of life." If anything good comes into our lives, he is the conduit.

And who are we? We are the branches. We bear fruit: "love, joy, peace, patience, kindness, goodness, faithfulness" (Gal. 5:22 NASB). We meditate on what is "true, and honorable, and right, and pure, and lovely, and admirable . . . excellent and worthy of praise" (Phil. 4:8 NLT). Our gentleness is evident to all. We bask in the "peace of God, which transcends all understanding" (Phil. 4:7 NIV).

And as we cling to Christ, God is honored. "My Father is glorified by this, that you bear much fruit, and so prove to be My disciples" (John 15:8 NASB).

———•———

The Father tends. Jesus nourishes. We receive, and grapes appear. Passersby, stunned at the overflowing baskets of love, grace, and peace, can't help but ask, "Who runs this vineyard?" And God is honored. For this reason fruit bearing matters to God.

And it matters to you! You grow weary of unrest. You're ready to be done with sleepless nights. You long to be "anxious for nothing." You long for the fruit of the Spirit. But how do you bear this fruit? Try harder? No, hang tighter. Our assignment is not fruitfulness but faithfulness. The secret to fruit bearing and anxiety-free living is less about doing and more about abiding.

Lest we miss this point, Jesus employs the word *abide(s)* ten times in seven verses:

Abide in Me, and I in you. As the branch cannot bear fruit of itself unless it *abides* in the vine, so neither can you unless you *abide* in Me. . . . he who *abides* in Me and I in him, he bears much fruit . . . If anyone does not *abide* in Me, he is thrown away as a branch and dries up . . . If you *abide* in Me, and My words *abide* in you, ask whatever you wish, and it will be done for you . . . *abide* in My love . . . *abide* in My love; just as I have kept My Father's commandments and *abide* in His love. (John 15:4–10 NASB)

"Come, live in me!" Jesus invites. "Make my home your home." Odds are that you know what it means to be at home somewhere.

To be at home is to feel safe. The residence is a place of refuge and security.

To be at home is to be comfortable. You can pad around wearing slippers and a robe.

To be at home is to be familiar. When you enter the door, you needn't consult the blueprint to find the kitchen.

Our aim—our only aim—is to be at home in Christ. He is not a roadside park or hotel room. He is our permanent mailing address. Christ is our home. He is our place of refuge and security. We are comfortable in his presence, free to be our authentic selves. We know our way around in him. We know his heart and his ways.

Our assignment is not fruitfulness but faithfulness.

We rest in him, find our nourishment in him. His roof of grace protects us from storms of guilt. His walls of providence secure us from destructive winds. His fireplace warms us during the lonely winters of life. We linger in the abode of Christ and never leave.

The branch never releases the vine. Ever! Does a branch show up on Sundays for its once-a-week meal? Only at the risk of death. The healthy branch never releases the vine, because there it receives nutrients twenty-four hours a day.

If branches had seminars, the topic would be "Secrets of Vine Grabbing." But branches don't have seminars, because to attend them they would have to release the vine—something they refuse to do. The dominant duty of the branch is to cling to the vine.

The dominant duty of the disciple is the same.

We Christians tend to miss this. We banter about pledges to "change the world," "make a difference for Christ," "lead people to the Lord." Yet these are by-products of the Christ-focused life. Our goal is not to bear fruit. Our goal is to stay attached.

Maybe this image will help. When a father leads his four-year-old son down a crowded street, he takes him by the hand and says, "Hold on to me." He doesn't say, "Memorize the map" or "Take your chances dodging the traffic" or "Let's see if you can find your way home." The good father gives the child one responsibility: "Hold on to my hand."

God does the same with us. Don't load yourself down with lists. Don't enhance your anxiety with the fear of not fulfilling them. Your goal is not to know every detail of the future. Your goal is to hold the hand of the One who does and never, ever let go.

This was the choice of Kent Brantly.

Brantly was a medical missionary in Liberia, waging a war on the cruelest of viruses, Ebola. The epidemic was killing people by the thousands. As much as any person in the world, Brantly knew the consequences of the disease. He had treated dozens of cases. He knew the symptoms—soaring fever, severe diarrhea, and nausea. He had seen the results of the virus, and for the first time he was feeling the symptoms himself.

His colleagues had drawn blood and begun the tests. But it would be at least three days before they knew the results. On Wednesday evening, July 23, 2014, Dr. Brantly quarantined himself in his house and waited. His wife and family were across the ocean. His coworkers could not enter his residence. He was, quite literally, alone with his thoughts. He opened his Bible and meditated on a passage from the book of Hebrews. Then he wrote in his journal, "The promise of entering his rest still stands, so let us never give up. Let us, therefore, make every effort . . . to enter that rest."[1]

Dr. Brantly considered the phrase "make every effort." He knew he would have to do exactly that. He then turned his attention to another verse from the same chapter in Hebrews: "Let us then approach the throne of grace with confidence, so that we may receive mercy and find grace to help us in our time of need."[2] He copied the scripture into his prayer journal and wrote the words "with confidence" in italics.[3]

He closed his journal and began the wait. The next three days brought unspeakable discomfort. The test results confirmed what they feared: he had contracted Ebola.

Kent's wife, Amber, was in her hometown of Abilene, Texas, when he called her with the diagnosis the following Saturday afternoon. She and their two children were visiting her parents. When her phone rang, she hurried to the bedroom for some privacy. Kent went straight to the point. "The test results came back. It's positive."

She began to cry. They talked for a few moments before Kent said that he was tired and would call again soon.

Now it was Amber's turn to process the news. She and her parents sat on the edge of her bed and wept for several minutes. After some time Amber excused herself and went outside. She walked across a field toward a large mesquite tree and took a seat on a low-hanging branch. She found it difficult to find words to formulate her prayers, so she used the lyrics of hymns she had learned as a young girl.

> There is no shadow of turning with Thee;
> Thou changest not, Thy compassions, they fail not
> As Thou hast been Thou forever wilt be.[4]

The words lifted her spirits, so she began to sing aloud another song she treasured:

> I need Thee every hour, in joy or pain;
> Come quickly and abide, or life is in vain.

I need Thee, O I need Thee;
Every hour I need Thee;
O bless me now, my Savior,
I come to Thee.[5]

She later wrote, "I thought my husband was going to die. I was in pain. I was afraid. Through those hymns, though, I was able to connect with God in a meaningful way when I couldn't find my own words to pray."[6]

Kent was transported from Africa to Atlanta. His caregivers chose to risk an untested treatment. Little by little his condition improved. Within a few days his strength began to return. The entire world, it seemed, rejoiced when he was able to exit the hospital, cured of Ebola.

We can applaud the Brantlys' victory over another disease, a virus that is every bit as deadly and contagious: the unseen contagion of anxiety. Kent and Amber were prime candidates for panic, yet they reacted with the same resolve that enabled them to battle Ebola. They stayed connected to the vine. They resolved to abide in Christ. Kent opened his Bible. Amber meditated on hymns. They filled their minds with the truth of God.

Jesus taught us to do the same. He tells us, rather bluntly, "Do not worry about your life, what you will eat or what you will drink; nor about your body, what you will put on" (Matt. 6:25).

He then gives two commands: "look" and "consider." He tells us to "look at the birds of the air" (Matt. 6:26). When we do, we notice how happy they seem to be. They aren't frowning, cranky, or grumpy. They don't appear sleep deprived or lonely. They sing, whistle, and soar. Yet "they neither sow nor reap nor gather into barns" (v. 26). They don't drive tractors or harvest wheat, yet Jesus asks us, do they appear well cared for?

He then turns our attention to the flowers of the field. "Consider the lilies" (v. 28). By the same token, they don't do anything. Even though their life span is short, God dresses them up for red-carpet appearances. Even Solomon, the richest king in history, "was not arrayed like one of these" (v. 29).

Saturate your heart with the goodness of God.

How do we disarm anxiety? Stockpile our minds with God thoughts. Draw the logical implication: if birds and flowers fall under the category of God's care, won't he care for us as well? Saturate your heart with the goodness of God.

"Set your mind on things above, not on things on the earth" (Col. 3:2).

How might you do this?

A friend recently described to me her daily ninety-minute commute.

"Ninety minutes!" I commiserated.

"Don't feel sorry for me." She smiled. "I use the trip to think about God." She went on to describe how she fills the hour and a half with worship and sermons. She listens to entire books of the Bible. She recites prayers. By the time she reaches her place of employment, she is ready for the day. "I turn my commute into my chapel."

Do something similar. Is there a block of time you can claim for God? Perhaps you could turn off the network news and open your Bible. Set the alarm fifteen minutes earlier. Or rather than watch the TV comedian as you fall asleep, listen to an audio version of a Christian book. "If you abide in my word, you are truly my disciples, and you will know the truth, and the truth will set you free" (John 8:31–32 ESV). Free from fear. Free from dread. And, yes, free from anxiety.

Chapter 11

C.A.L.M.

Choose the tranquili-tree over the anxie-tree.

It's two thirty in the morning. You can't sleep. You pound your pillow, adjust the blankets. You roll on this side, then the other. Nothing works. Everyone else sleeps. Your spouse has taken up residence in dreamland. The dog is curled up in a lump at the foot of your bed. Everyone is asleep. Everyone, that is, except you.

In six hours you'll be walking into a new job, new office, new chapter, new world. You'll be the rookie on the sales team. You are wondering if you made the right decision. The hours are long. The economy is declining. The competition is increasing.

Besides, you are

- twenty-three years old, right out of college, starting your first job;
- thirty-three years old, with two kids to feed and a family to care for;
- forty-three years old, the latest victim of layoffs and downsizing;
- fifty-three years old, not the ideal age to change careers;
- sixty-three years old. What happened to retirement plans and time with the grandkids? Here you are starting over.

No matter the age, questions fall like hailstones. Will I make enough money? Make any friends? Have a cubicle? Will I be able to learn the software program, the sales pitch, the way to the restroom?

You feel a twitch in the back of your neck. Suddenly a new strand of anxiety worms its way into your mind. *Oh no, a tumor. Just like Granddad. He spent a year in chemotherapy. How will I endure chemo and a new job? Will my insurance cover chemo?*

The thoughts rage through your mind like a tornado through a Kansas prairie. They suck any vestige of peace into the sky. The green numbers on the clock are the only lights in your room, indeed the only lights in your life. Another hour passes. You cover your head with a pillow and feel like crying.

What a mess.

What does all this anxiety mean? All this fear? Trepidation? Restlessness? Insecurity? What does it mean?

Simply this: you are a human.

It does not mean you are emotionally underdeveloped. It does not mean you are stupid, demon possessed, or a failure. It does not mean your parents failed you or vice versa. And, this is important, it does not mean you are not a Christian.

Christians battle anxiety. Jesus battled anxiety, for heaven's sake! In the Garden of Gethsemane he prayed three times that he wouldn't have to drink of the cup (Matt. 26:36–44). His heart pumped with such ferocity that capillaries broke and rivulets of crimson streaked down his face (Luke 22:44). He was anxious.

But he didn't stay anxious. He entrusted his fears to his heavenly Father and completed his earthly mission with faith. He will help us do likewise. There is a pathway out of the valley of fret. God used the pen of Paul to sketch the map.

> Rejoice in the Lord always. Again I will say, rejoice!
>
> Let your gentleness be known to all men. The Lord is at hand.

Be anxious for nothing, but in everything by prayer and supplication, with thanksgiving, let your requests be made known to God; and the peace of God, which surpasses all understanding, will guard your hearts and minds through Christ Jesus.

Finally, brethren, whatever things are true, whatever things are noble, whatever things are just, whatever things are pure, whatever things are lovely, whatever things are of good report, if there is any virtue and if there is anything praiseworthy—meditate on these things. (Phil. 4:4–8)

A person would be hard-pressed to find a more practical, powerful, and inspirational passage on the topic of anxiety. The passage has the feel of a "decision tree." A decision tree is a tool that uses a treelike graph to show decisions and their possible consequences. Paul's counsel has a similar sequential format.

You already know about the anxie-tree. We've spent more than our share of time dangling from its wimpy branches, whipped about by the winds of change and turmoil. On one occasion God sent the prophet Isaiah to soothe the concerns of an anxious king. He and his people were so frightened that "they shook with fear like trees of the forest blown by the wind" (Isa. 7:2 NCV). Sounds as if they were sitting in a grove of anxie-trees. God gave this word to Isaiah: "Tell Ahaz, 'Be careful. Be calm and don't worry'" (Isa. 7:4 NCV).

The anxie-tree is not the only tree in the orchard. There is a better option: the tranquili-tree. (Aren't I clever?) It is sturdy, shady, and has ample room for you. Here is how you use it.

Begin with God.

Celebrate God's goodness. "Rejoice in the Lord always. Again I will say, rejoice!" (Phil. 4:4). Turn your attention away from the problem, and for a few minutes celebrate God. It does you no good to obsess

———•———

yourself with your trouble. The more you stare at it, the bigger it grows. Yet the more you look to God, the quicker the problem is reduced to its proper size. This was the strategy of the psalmist.

> I will lift up my eyes to the hills—
> From whence comes my help?
> My help comes from the LORD,
> Who made heaven and earth. (Ps. 121:1–2)

Do you see the intentionality in those words? "I will lift up my eyes." Do not meditate on the mess. You gain nothing by setting your eyes on the problem. You gain everything by setting your eyes on the Lord.

Do not meditate on the mess.

This was the lesson Peter learned on the stormy Sea of Galilee. He was a fisherman. He knew what ten-foot waves could do to small boats. Maybe that is why he volunteered to leave the craft when he saw Jesus walking on the water through the storm.

> Peter said, "Lord, if it is really you, then command me to come to you on the water."
> Jesus said, "Come."
> And Peter left the boat and walked on the water to Jesus. But when Peter saw the wind and the waves, he became afraid and began to sink. He shouted, "Lord, save me!" (Matt. 14:28–30 NCV)

As long as Peter focused on the face of Christ, he did the impossible. Yet when he shifted his gaze to the force of the storm, he sank like a stone. If you are sinking, it is because you are looking in the wrong direction.

Is God sovereign over your circumstances? Is he mightier than your problem? Does he have answers to your questions? According to the Bible the answer is yes, yes, and yes! "God . . . is the blessed controller of all things, the king over all kings and the master of all masters" (1 Tim. 6:15 PHILLIPS).

If he sustains all and controls all, do you think he has authority over this situation you face?

What about his mercy? Is God's grace great enough to cover your sin? Again, yes! "There is now no condemnation for those who are in Christ Jesus" (Rom. 8:1 NIV).

1. **Rejoice in the Lord.** This is step one. Do not hurry past it. Face God before you face your problem. Then you will be ready to . . .

2. *Ask God for help.* "Let your requests be made known to God" (Phil. 4:6). Fear triggers either despair or prayer. Choose wisely.

God said, "Call on me in the day of trouble" (Ps. 50:15 NIV).

Jesus said, "Ask, and it will be given to you; seek, and you will find; knock, and it will be opened to you" (Matt. 7:7). There is no uncertainty in that promise. No "might," "perhaps," or "possibly will." Jesus states unflinchingly that when you ask, he listens.

So ask! When anxiety knocks on the door, say, "Jesus, would you mind answering that?" Reduce your request to one statement. Imitate Jesus, who taught us to pray, "Give us this day our daily bread" (Matt. 6:11). Engage in specific prayer. And engage in promise-based prayer. Stand on the firm foundation of God's covenant. "Let us then approach God's throne of grace with confidence" (Heb. 4:16 NIV).

Having done so . . .

3. *Leave your concerns with God.* Let him take charge. Let God do what he is so willing to do: "Guard your hearts and minds through Christ Jesus" (Phil. 4:7).

Have you ever left an appliance at the repair shop? Perhaps your toaster broke or your microwave oven stopped working. You tried to fix it but had no success. So you took it to the specialist. You explained the problem and then . . .

- offered to stay and help him fix it,
- hovered next to his workbench asking questions about the progress,
- threw a sleeping bag on the floor of the workshop so you could watch the repairman at work.

If you did any of these things, you don't understand the relationship between client and repairman. The arrangement is uncomplicated. Leave it with him to fix it. Our protocol with God is equally simple. Leave your problem with him. "I know whom I have believed and am persuaded that He is able to keep what I have committed to Him until that Day" (2 Tim. 1:12).

God does not need our help, counsel, or assistance. (Please repeat this phrase: I hereby resign as ruler of the universe.) When he is ready for us to reengage, he will let us know.

Until then, replace anxious thoughts with grateful ones. God takes thanksgiving seriously.

Here's why: gratitude keeps us focused on the present.

The Bible's most common word for *worry* is the Greek term *merimnate*. The origin is *merimnaō*. This is a compound of a verb and a noun. The verb is *divide*. The noun is *mind*. To be anxious, then, is to divide the mind.[1] Worry takes a meat cleaver to our thoughts, energy, and focus. Anxiety chops up our attention. It sends our awareness in a dozen directions.

We worry about the past—what we said or did. We worry about the future—tomorrow's assignments or the next decade's developments. Anxiety takes our attention from the right now and directs it "back then" or "out there."

But when you aren't focused on your problem, you have a sudden availability of brain space. Use it for good.

4. *Meditate on good things.* "Finally, brethren, whatever things are true, whatever things are noble, whatever things are just, whatever things are pure, whatever things are lovely, whatever things are of good report, if there is any virtue and if there is anything praiseworthy— meditate on these things" (Phil. 4:8). Don't let anxious, negative thoughts take over your mind. You cannot control the circumstances, but you can always control what you think of them.

Gratitude keeps us focused on the present.

One of the toughest days of my life found me in a diner in Dalton, Georgia. I was nineteen years old and one week into my first summer of college. I was a thousand miles from home. I was sleeping at the Salvation Army shelter where, the night before, an inebriated guy on the bunk above mine rolled over and puked. If homesickness were water, I would have been soaked to the bone.

On the promise of fast cash and new sights, I'd joined up with two friends and signed on to sell books door-to-door. My friends went home during sales school. I was all alone. I went to the field and made this discovery: no one likes a door-to-door salesman. My first day was miserable.

"Hello, I'm Max . . ." Slam.

"Hello, I'm Max . . ." Slam.

"Hello, I'm Max . . ." Slam.

Day two wasn't any better. I was lower than a snake's belly. At lunch I dragged myself into a diner, nursed my bruised ego, and ate a hamburger. As I was paying my bill, I spotted a display of magnetized, rubberized truisms adjacent to the cash register. One was yellow, shaped like a lemon, and contained these words: "When life gives you a lemon, make lemonade."

The slogan was folksy, corny, and homespun. But I had never heard it. And it was just enough to convince me to keep at the job. I bought the magnet and affixed it to a metal strip on the dashboard of my '73 Plymouth Duster. Whenever I got discouraged, I would rub my thumb over the rubber lemon and remind myself, *I can make myself miserable, or I can make myself some lemonade.*

People still slammed doors, and I still wondered what in the world I was doing so far from home. But I survived.

It's been four decades since that day in the diner. Much has changed. But this much hasn't: life still gives lemons.

Of course, my prospects of a miserable summer are nothing compared to the lemons you've been handed. Just recently I spoke with an elderly woman whose husband has been diagnosed with dementia. She needs to take away his car keys. I spoke with a single mom who can't remember her last good night of sleep. She wonders if she has what it takes to raise kids. I spoke to a middle-aged man who is reeling from the consequences of a divorce. He wonders if he'll ever have a happy family.

Life still gives lemons. Life gives lemons to good people, bad people, old people, all people. Life comes with lemons.

But we don't have to suck on them.

I once wrote this resolve:

---·---

Life gives lemons to good people,

bad people, old people, all people.

Life comes with lemons. But we

don't have to suck on them.

---·---

Today, I will live today.

Yesterday has passed.

Tomorrow is not yet.

I'm left with today.

So, today, I will live today.

Relive yesterday? No.

I will learn from it.

I will seek mercy for it.

I will take joy in it.

But I won't live in it.

The sun has set on yesterday.

The sun has yet to rise on tomorrow.

Worry about the future? To what gain?

It deserves a glance, nothing more.

I can't change tomorrow until tomorrow.

Today, I will live today.

I will face today's challenges with today's strength.

I will dance today's waltz with today's music.

I will celebrate today's opportunities with today's hope.

Today.

May I laugh, listen, learn, and love. And tomorrow, if it comes, may I do so again.

A new day awaits you, my friend. A new season in which you will worry less and trust more. A season with reduced fear and enhanced faith. Can you imagine a life in which you are anxious for nothing? God can. And, with his help, you will experience it.

———•———

QUESTIONS FOR REFLECTION

Prepared by Jessalyn Foggy

Chapter 1

LESS FRET, MORE FAITH

Read Philippians 4:4–9

CONFRONT THE CHAOS

1. Max lists several descriptors of anxiety: "a low-grade fear," "edginess," and "a free-floating sense of dread," to name a few.

   - Even if you've never considered yourself to be someone who struggles with anxiety, did any of these descriptions ring true for you? If so, which one(s)?
   - If you have recognized anxiety as part of your life for a while now, which aspect did you relate to the most? Why?

2. Define *anxiety* in your own words based on your experiences. What role does anxiety play in your life?

3. "Anxiety and fear are cousins but not twins." Do you agree? If so, how do the two manifest themselves differently in your life?

4. Take some time to define your personal anxieties.

   - What keeps you awake at night or wakes you up early?
   - What persistently distracts you from the task at hand?
   - What makes your chest tighten?
   - If your anxieties change day to day, focus on naming what is currently on your mind and heart.

Choose Calm

5. Consider this: "We have been taught that the Christian life is a life of peace, and when we don't have peace, we assume the problem lies within us." If this has been your perspective, how does Philippians 4:4–9 make you feel?

   - Does it motivate you?
   - Does it discourage you?
   - Does it feel impossible?

6. "Anxiety is not a sin; it is an emotion." Chapter 1 points out four consistent causes of anxiety: change, pace of life, personal challenges, and aging.

   - Think of a time when change created anxiety in your life. What is it about the nature of change that lends itself to anxiety?
   - Consider your current pace of life. Do you live in survival mode? If so, how many items or events on your to-do list do you say yes to out of obligation or a "need to be needed"? Is there something you could say no to that would create some margin in your life? Why or why not?
   - Personal challenges can include many different things, but they are often concerns that stick around for a while, perhaps even for a lifetime. That means it's important to address them. What are some personal challenges that cause you to worry? Are these concerns outside of your control? If so, are you praying about these issues daily?
   - What scares you most about getting older? Consider how the Bible talks about age (Prov. 16:31; Isa. 46:4; Job 12:12). Do these verses sound different from the way we as a society talk about aging? If so, how?

7. Read the following passages and note the promise held in each:

> Trust in the LORD with all your heart,
> And lean not on your own understanding;
> In all your ways acknowledge Him,
> And He shall direct your paths.
>
> —PROVERBS 3:5–6

> "Come to Me, all you who labor and are heavy laden, and I will give you rest. Take My yoke upon you and learn from Me, for I am gentle and lowly in heart, and you will find rest for your souls. For My yoke is easy and My burden is light."
>
> —MATTHEW 11:28–30

> "Peace I leave with you, My peace I give to you; not as the world gives do I give to you. Let not your heart be troubled, neither let it be afraid."
>
> —JOHN 14:27

> Cast your burden on the LORD,
> And He shall sustain you;
> He shall never permit the righteous to be moved.
>
> —PSALM 55:22

> Therefore humble yourselves under the mighty hand of God, that He may exalt you in due time, casting all your care upon Him, for He cares for you.
>
> —1 PETER 5:6–7

> Yea, though I walk through the valley of the shadow of death,
> I will fear no evil;
> For You are with me;

Your rod and Your staff, they comfort me.

—Psalm 23:4

- How can these promises change your outlook on the day ahead?
- What do these promises say about God's power compared to the anxieties that you face?

8. Write down the C.A.L.M. acronym, and place it somewhere accessible to remind yourself that "the peace of God, which surpasses all understanding, will guard your hearts and minds."

CELEBRATE God's goodness.

"Rejoice in the Lord always" (Phil. 4:4).

- How will you express your joy for God's goodness today?

ASK God for help.

"Let your requests be made known to God" (v. 6).

- If you don't already keep a prayer journal, start one. Begin with today's requests.

LEAVE your concerns with him.

"With thanksgiving . . ." (v. 6).

- At bedtime review the concerns you left with God this morning. Thank him for relieving you of your anxious thoughts.

MEDITATE on good things.

"Think about the things that are good and worthy of praise" (v. 8 NCV).

- Plan your day to include time alone with God.

MEDITATION

Dear Lord,

You spoke to storms. Would you speak to ours? You calmed the hearts of the apostles. Would you calm the chaos within us? You told them to fear not. Say the same to us. We are weary from our worry, battered and belittled by the gales of life. Oh Prince of Peace, bequeath to us a spirit of calm. As we turn the page in this book, will you turn a new leaf in our lives? Quench anxiety. Stir courage. Let us know less fret and more faith.

In Jesus' name, amen.

Chapter 2

REJOICE IN THE LORD'S SOVEREIGNTY

*You can't run the world, but you
can entrust it to God.*

Read Isaiah 6

CONFRONT THE CHAOS

1. What pictures, images, or people come to mind when you hear the word *sovereign*?

2. Consider what *sovereign* means in your everyday life. Do you believe you have yielded sovereignty to God?

   - If not, why?
   - If yes, do you also *trust* his sovereignty?

3. This chapter emphasizes the concept that "belief always precedes behavior." Your mind is the rudder of your actions.

   - What did you learn in this chapter about your belief system?
   - Does your behavior reflect a sturdy belief system? Why or why not?

4. There are many things that might make it hard to trust in the goodness of God's sovereignty. Read 2 Corinthians 11:23–29, Paul's

---

long list of perils. Then read in Philippians 1:12–13 Paul's response
to his circumstances.

- In what circumstances do you struggle to trust God's purposes?
- Do you feel that God is fair in asking for a pure response like
  Paul's? Why or why not?
- What keeps you from fully believing that God is a good Father
  who cares for every detail of your life?
- Take the time to bring these obstacles before the Lord and pray,
  "Lord, I believe; help my unbelief!" (Mark 9:24).

5. Hebrews 13:7–8 says, "Remember your leaders. . . . Consider the
   outcome of their way of life, and imitate their faith. Jesus Christ is
   the same yesterday and today and forever" (ESV).

- Are there people in your life who believed in the steady hand of
  God when they had much to be anxious about? How did it turn
  out for them?
- How might their examples affect your capacity for trusting
  God's sovereignty?
- Read Hebrews 11 and meditate on the many faithful who
  experienced both blessings and hardships in this life, who
  trusted the immutable God we struggle to trust today. How did
  their stories conclude? Was trusting in God worth it for them?
  Why or why not?
- How can you use these stories as ammunition against anxiety?

Choose Calm

6. Ponder this statement: "The mind cannot at the same time be full
   of God and full of fear."

- How might this truth affect how you spend your free time?

- What action steps can you take to discipline your mind?

7. "Your anxiety decreases as your understanding of your father increases." Putting this thought into practice, in what ways can you pursue a deeper understanding of who God is?

   - What intentional changes can you make in your daily schedule to ensure that God's character is at the forefront of your mind?
   - How would your demeanor change if you would "dare to believe that good things will happen"?

8. Hear this challenge today: "Are you troubled, restless, sleepless? Then rejoice in the Lord's sovereignty. I dare you—I double-dog dare you—to expose your worries to an hour of worship. Your concerns will melt like ice on a July sidewalk. Anxiety passes as trust increases."

   This week take Max up on the challenge to expose your worries to an hour of worship.

MEDITATION

PRAYER OF SAINT PATRICK

I arise today
Through the strength of heaven;
Light of the sun,
Splendor of fire,
Speed of lightning,
Swiftness of the wind,
Depth of the sea,
Stability of the earth,
Firmness of the rock.

I arise today
Through God's strength to pilot me;
God's might to uphold me,
God's wisdom to guide me,

I arise today
Through the mighty strength
Of the Lord of creation.[1]

Chapter 3

REJOICE IN THE
LORD'S MERCY

Guilt frenzies the soul. Grace calms it.

CONFRONT THE CHAOS

1. "There is a guilt that sits in the soul like a concrete block and causes a person to feel bad for being alive. There is a guilt that says, *I did bad.* And then there is a guilt that concludes, *I am bad.* It was this deep, dark guilt that I felt. I found myself face-to-face with a version of me I had never known."

   - Can you relate to this disorienting, dark guilt described above?
   - Perhaps your guilt is triggered by an event in the past, or maybe it is prompted by something you daily struggle to overcome. Take time to think through and identify the most cavernous sources of guilt in your life.

2. Read Genesis 3, the account of sin entering the world. As you read, list the emotions Adam and Eve experienced immediately after they disobeyed.

   - When did the negative feelings start?
   - How did Adam and Eve move from negative thinking to sinful action?

---·---

- Note how they reacted emotionally and physically.

3. "Lists of anxiety triggers typically include busy schedules, unrealistic demands, or heavy traffic. But we must go deeper. Behind the frantic expressions on the faces of humanity is unresolved regret."

   - Do you agree with the above statement? Why or why not?
   - Was this statement true for Adam and Eve?
   - Could something deeper than heavy traffic and business demands be causing your anxiety?
   - Would you attribute part of what you feel to regret or guilt? Why or why not?

4. Pages 39–40 list the ways we try to process our guilt and failure. *Numb, deny, minimize, bury, punish, avoid, redirect, offset,* and *embody* are the main false approaches described. Reread their descriptions in chapter 3.

   - During times of high anxiety, which of these false approaches do you indulge in most often?
   - Refer to your answers to question 1. How do you try to process the deepest parts of your guilt?

5. Confronting our guilt is unpleasant because it often requires us to relive painful experiences or seasons of our lives. But not addressing guilt only perpetuates the problem. "Unresolved guilt will turn you into a miserable, weary, angry, stressed-out, fretful mess."

   - Examine your guilt. Are you burdened because you need to ask forgiveness of someone? Come up with a plan to do so. Make the call. Write the note. Unburden your heart.

- Read Psalm 32:3–4 again. Can you relate? Are your anxiety and fear taking a toll on you physically? Explain.
- Do you feel as if you are always running, always hiding?
- If the answer is yes, choose someone to confess these feelings to this week. Entrust these secrets to someone who is worthy of trust. When we say something aloud, it often loses some of its power over our minds.

CHOOSE CALM

6. So where do we go from here? Once we have identified our guilt, how do we move forward in a healthy way? There is good news for those who can address their chaos head-on:

> "A happy saint is one who is at the same time *aware of the severity of sin* and the *immensity of grace*. Sin is not diminished, nor is God's ability to forgive it. The saint dwells in grace, not guilt. This is the tranquil soul."

- Do you think that acknowledging the severity of your sin increases the gloriousness and power of the news that grace is available to you? Why or why not?
- Additionally, can you identify the role of choice in the quotation above? What is your role?

7. "My salvation has nothing to do with my work and everything to do with the finished work of Christ on the cross."
- Do you believe this is true? If so, do you live as if this is true? How or how not?
- If you don't believe this, "we have stumbled upon a source of your anxiety. . . . What you did was not good. But your God

is good. And he will forgive you. He is ready to write a new chapter in your life. Say with Paul, 'Forgetting the past and looking forward to what lies ahead, I strain to reach the end of the race and receive the prize for which God is calling us' (Phil. 3:13–14 TLB)."

- Take time to write a prayer asking God to help you believe that his grace is truly greater than whatever you have done.

8. Chapter 3 concludes with the story of a trapeze artist. Reread the story and the metaphor Max draws from it.
   - What holds you back from fully trusting God to catch you?
   - While it may seem unnatural to "practice" trust, we shouldn't be surprised that it requires disciplined effort. The Bible repeatedly refers to the faith journey with athletic metaphors, insinuating that it takes daily dedication and discipline to train our minds and hearts. What are some practical ways you can discipline your mind and heart to release your guilt to the Lord each day?

MEDITATION

"Your Father has never dropped anyone. He will not drop you. His grip is sturdy and his hands are open. As the apostle Paul proclaimed, 'And *I know* the Lord will continue to rescue me from every *trip, trap, snare, and pitfall of* evil and carry me safely to His heavenly kingdom. May He be glorified throughout eternity. Amen.'"[22]

Chapter 4

REJOICE IN THE
LORD *ALWAYS*

God uses everything to accomplish his will.

Read Genesis 39–40

CONFRONT THE CHAOS

1. Joseph encountered setback after setback. Even before he suffered injustice from Potiphar's wife and neglect in prison, Joseph was sold by his own brothers into slavery. Few people have been more "forgotten."

   - Do you feel forgotten? In what areas of your life is this most poignant?
   - How does the command to "rejoice in the Lord always" (Phil. 4:4) make you feel? (It's okay to be honest if it makes you angry or feel misunderstood!)

2. Max briefly reviews different belief systems for how God interacts with the created world. "Is [God] aware? Does he care? Deism says no. God created the universe and then abandoned it. Pantheism says no. Creation has no story or purpose unto itself; it is only a part of God. Atheism says no. Not surprisingly, the philosophy that dismisses the existence of a god will, in turn, dismiss the possibility

of a divine plan. Christianity, on the other hand, says, 'Yes, there is a God. Yes, this God is personally and powerfully involved in his creation.'" How you see God interacting with his creation is crucial to your feelings toward him in hard circumstances.

- How would you describe God's interaction with creation?
- What do you base this on?

3. "'He is before all things, and in him all things hold together' (Col. 1:17 NIV). Were he to step back, the creation would collapse. His resignation would spell our evaporation. 'For in him we live and move and have our being' (Acts 17:28 NIV)."

- Read Colossians 1 and Acts 17.
- How do they inform your theology of God's participation in our daily lives?

4. From what we read of Joseph, he seemed to be repeatedly faithful despite the difficult circumstances that consistently followed him.

- Why do you think God allowed Joseph to endure rejection, injustice, and loss—not just once, but repeatedly?
- Have you ever responded like Joseph and yet felt as if God allowed so much pain that good couldn't come from it? If so, how did that shape your view of God's character?
- Do you think that staying faithful deserves a reward? Does God owe you for your perseverance? Be honest with yourself. Why or why not?

5. Think about your life and the lives of other believers you know. Has any good come from terrible circumstances?

- Take one such circumstance, and make a list of any light that has come from the darkness of the situation.

- How do you reconcile tragedies in the news with your understanding of a loving God?

CHOOSE CALM

6. The ability to "rejoice always" *must* come from something outside our sphere of experience. Life is too hard and too painful to supply enough temporary moments of elation to sustain the ability to *rejoice always*. If Joseph had decided to rejoice always based on his brief experiences of joy, it never would have lasted.

    - It's all about perspective. Are you placing an inordinate amount of your affection, identity, and purpose in something you may lose?

    - If you believe in Jesus and are considered a child of God, this life is miniscule in comparison to eternity. How can you refocus your attention and direct your affection, identity, and purpose toward what is to come?

    - Does the concept of an eternity with no pain, hurt, or loss give you consolation for this life and whatever you are facing here and now? Does this future you are promised create any joy in your soul? Why or why not?

7. Refer back to question 1. With the reminder of the things that make you feel forgotten, read these scriptures:

    Isaiah 49:15–16

    Isaiah 53

    - If God was willing to give his own Son to die on our behalf, do you really believe he has forgotten you? If Jesus was willing to endure for you every affliction known to humanity, do you really believe your trials (excruciating as they may be) are because he does not love you?

- Sometimes tragedy makes no sense. We may have to wait for eternity to know the answer to the question *why*. But we do know he loves us and has engraved us on the palm of his hands. Take time to meditate on this truth.

8. Rejoicing doesn't always look like what we may think. It doesn't have to be a smiling face and an upbeat personality.
   - Read 2 Corinthians 6:4–10.
   - Write in your own words what it means to rejoice always.

9. Each day presents an opportunity to choose. "If the story of Joseph teaches us anything, it is this: we have a choice. We can wear our hurt or wear our hope. We can outfit ourselves in our misfortune, or we can clothe ourselves in God's providence. We can cave in to the pandemonium of life, or we can lean into the perfect plan of God. And we can believe this promise: 'In all things God works for the good of those who love him, who have been called according to his purpose' (Rom. 8:28 NIV)."
   - How can you make it a point to choose hope? What do you need to relinquish to do this?
   - Anxiety will come, but when it comes, what will you choose to rejoice over?

MEDITATION

IT IS WELL WITH MY SOUL

When peace, like a river, attendeth my way,
When sorrows like sea billows roll;

Whatever my lot, Thou hast taught me to say,
It is well, it is well with my soul.

Though Satan should buffet, though trials should come,
Let this blest assurance control,
That Christ hath regarded my helpless estate,
And hath shed His own blood for my soul.

My sin—oh, the bliss of this glorious thought!—
My sin, not in part but the whole,
Is nailed to the cross, and I bear it no more,
Praise the Lord, praise the Lord, O my soul!

And Lord, haste the day when the faith shall be sight,
The clouds be rolled back as a scroll;
The trump shall resound, and the Lord shall descend,
Even so, it is well with my soul.

It is well with my soul,
It is well, it is well with my soul.[3]

Chapter 5

CONTAGIOUS CALM

Anxiety is needless because God is near.

CONFRONT THE CHAOS

1. Consider this statement: "You will be tempted to press the button and release, not nuclear warheads, but angry outbursts, a rash of accusations, a fiery retaliation of hurtful words. Unchecked anxiety unleashes an Enola Gay of destruction. How many people have been wounded as a result of unbridled stress?"

   - How do you react to the unexpected?
   - Would those close to you describe you as "seasoned and mature"? Why or why not?
   - What causes you to react or respond with an unbridled temper?
   - Do you feel that you are able to control your instinctual reactions in moments that quickly spiral downward? If so, what helps you do this?

2. Do you know people who are characterized by calm?

   - How do those people make you feel?
   - Do you enjoy being around them?
   - How do other people respond or interact with them?
   - What other qualities and character traits do they have that stem from their contagious calm?

———•———

173

- Think of a time you witnessed a stressful situation that was resolved because a person reacted calmly.

3. Read the account of Jesus feeding the five thousand in all four of the gospels (Matt. 14:13–21; Mark 6:30–44; Luke 9:10–17; John 6:1–15).

   - Notice the disciples' gut reaction in each account. How did they respond?
   - Put yourself in their shoes. Imagine fifty people unexpectedly showing up for dinner at your house. Consider not what you would *do* but how you would *react*. Explain.

4. Anxiety increases when we feel we are losing control. This is amplified when we feel that everything is up to us or we are the only ones who can fix a situation. Hence, anxiety is amplified when we feel alone.

   - When do you feel most alone?
   - Is it a situation, person, experience, or a season of life that causes you to feel alone?
   - Is there someone you go to when you feel alone?
   - Has that person ever let you down? Or worse, has that person ever made the loneliness greater?

Choose Calm

5. When others have let us down, the friendship of the Lord is sweetest. Read Psalm 25:14.

   - Do you have a *friendship* with the Lord?
   - How could viewing the Lord as a faithful friend who greets you in the early morning for a long walk or a conversation over

coffee shape the way you see your current situation?
- Take time to meet with the Lord as a friend this week. Rest, knowing he sees and he feels along with you more than anyone else in your life can.

6. To feel truly known and understood by another human is rare; indeed, it is a luxury, not a birthright.

- Read Psalm 139 and list the ways it states that God knows you.
- Based on this passage, is there anything he wouldn't understand about you? How does that knowledge affect your prayers?

In our loneliest moments the One who formed our "inmost being and knitted us together in the womb" offers us a friendship, a nearness unlike any other. God created our inmost and our outermost beings. He knows us emotionally, physically, and mentally better than anyone else.

7. Read this definition of calm: "For the righteous will never be moved; he will be remembered forever. He is not afraid of bad news; his heart is firm, trusting in the LORD. His heart is steady" (Ps. 112:6–8 ESV).

- According to this verse, where does steadiness originate?
- Ask the Lord for greater trust in the nearness of his presence today.

MEDITATION

In the ultimate declaration of communion, God called himself Immanuel, which means "God with us." He became flesh. He became sin. He defeated the grave. He is still with us. In the form of his Spirit, he comforts, teaches, and convicts. Do not assume God is watching from a distance. Avoid the quicksand that bears the marker "God has left you!" Do not indulge this lie. If you do, your problem will be amplified by a sense of loneliness. It's one thing to face a challenge, but to face it all alone? Isolation creates a downward cycle of fret. Choose instead to be the person who clutches the presence of God with both hands. "The LORD is with me; I will not be afraid. What can mere mortals do to me?" (Ps. 118:6 NIV).

Chapter 6

PRAYER, NOT DESPAIR

Peace happens when people pray.

CONFRONT THE CHAOS

1. Think through your attitude toward prayer. Maybe you have been a Christian for a very long time and prayer has become trite. Maybe you are a new Christian and you are overwhelmed by this awe-inspiring interaction.

   - Are you jaded, confused, or apathetic, or are you excited about prayer?
   - Try to describe your prayer life in one phrase.

2. Read the parable of contrast in Luke 18:1–8 referred to in the beginning of chapter 6.

   - Read through the verses again, and note the differences between you and the widow in one column and the differences between God and the judge in another column.
   - What do you think it says about the nature of prayer that Jesus knew we would need a story that inspires us to pray consistently and never quit?
   - What is the one characteristic or posture that dominates this parable? What attribute of the praying life is most emphasized?

3. The parable ends with the question "Nevertheless, when the Son of Man comes, will He really find faith on the earth?"

   - What does this imply?
   - How would you answer this question?

4. "God doesn't delay. He never places you on hold or tells you to call again later. God loves the sound of your voice. Always. He doesn't hide when you call. He hears your prayers."

   - Is it hard for you to believe that God wants to hear your prayers? Why or why not?
   - Is there an experience or situation that has deeply influenced this opinion? Explain.
   - If you knew for certain that God was listening to your prayers, how would your prayer life change?

5. Read the end of Luke 18, verses 35–43. As is characteristic of Jesus' healings, he says to the blind man, "Your faith has made you well."

   - How is the blind man's faith evident in this interaction? Look carefully at the words used in this passage.
   - Notice also the crowd in the story. What is their reaction before the healing? What is their reaction after the healing?
   - Have you ever felt alone in your belief in the power of prayer?
   - Does popular opinion sway your belief in the power of prayer?
   - What might this story say about the effect your prayer life can have on those around you?

CHOOSE CALM

6. Max notes the benefits of a *specific* prayer in chapter 6. A specific

prayer is "a serious prayer" and "an opportunity for us to see God at work," and it "creates a lighter load."

- Consider your anxieties. Do you bring them, specifically, to God in prayer?
- If yes, how? If no, how might you do this?

7. Prayer takes discipline and dedication. It takes effort to make the time, and it takes belief to be consistent. If we don't believe that God is hearing us or that he cares, our determination to pray will quickly fade.

> "Therefore humble yourselves under the mighty hand of God, that He may exalt you in due time, casting all your care upon Him, for He cares for you" (1 Peter 5:6–7).

- According to these verses, why should you give your anxieties to God?
- Is this a good enough reason to put the effort into prayer?
- Notice, this verse does not ask you to forget or set side your anxieties. It acknowledges that your anxieties are real. Instead of pushing them aside, you are putting them literally *on* God. He tells you to transfer the burden from yourself to him. How might this imagery guide the way you pray?
- Determine a time each day when you will choose to list your anxieties. Physically fold up the list and place it somewhere (in a basket, drawer, etc.). When you start to feel anxious, remember that you have placed your burdens on God for the day.

8. In your own Bible reading, find three of God's promises that speak to you. Hold God to his word, and ask him to do that which he has already said he would do in your life.

MEDITATION

"Come to me, all of you who are weary and carry heavy burdens, and I will give you rest. Take my yoke upon you. Let me teach you, because I am humble and gentle at heart, and you will find rest for your souls. For my yoke is easy to bear, and the burden I give you is light" (Matt. 11:28–30 NLT).

Chapter 7

GREAT GRATITUDE

Christ-based contentment turns
us into strong people.

CONFRONT THE CHAOS

1. Consider this question, "Does it seem the good life is always one *if only* away? One purchase away? One promotion away? One election, transition, or romance away?"

   - What's the *if only* you have been distracted by lately? Sometimes the things we desire are good but our obsession with getting them becomes consuming. Good things turn into bad things when they become ultimate things.
   - Is your *if only* a good thing, in and of itself? If so, is your dedication to it dangerous?

2. What practices have you instituted to chase after your *if only*?

   - Are these practices healthy?
   - Why or why not?

3. Take some time to look at your calendar from the past month. Then, take some time to read your journal, or if you don't keep a journal, review what distracts you throughout the day.

   - How did you spend most of your time?

---·---

- How do you spend your mental energy?
- Do you notice a pattern? Are there certain things that tend to occupy your time, thoughts, and resources? What does this say about your idea of where to find "the good life"?

4. Do you resonate with this description: "You're in a hurry to cross the [If Only] river and worried that you never will"?

   - Do you have a plan for your life that you fear may never happen?
   - If this dream were never to come true, could you still find value in life? Why or why not?

CHOOSE CALM

5. Chapter 7 talks about two lists: the list of *if only* and the list of *already*. You described your *if only*s in question 1. Take time now to write down your *already*s.

   - What are some things for which you are grateful?
   - What are some things you thought might never happen that have been given to you?

6. Read Philippians 4:11–13. "Paul's use of the term *secret* is curious. He doesn't say, 'I have learned the *principle*.' Or 'I have learned the *concept*.' Instead, 'I have learned the *secret* of being content.'"

   - Why do you think it is so hard to be content?
   - Do you think it is possible for you to find what Paul found— contentment no matter what happened?

7. Contingent contentment sounds tiring and anxiety producing.

   - If you kept your focus on gifts that you already have and that you cannot lose, how might your attitude change?

- How would your relationships change?

MEDITATION

"Death, failure, betrayal, sickness, disappointment—they cannot take our joy, because they cannot take our Jesus. What you have in Christ is greater than anything you don't have in life. You have God, who is crazy about you, and the forces of heaven to monitor and protect you. You have the living presence of Jesus within you. In Christ you have everything."

Chapter 8

GOD'S PEACE, YOUR PEACE

*You may be facing the perfect storm,
but Jesus offers the perfect peace.*

CONFRONT THE CHAOS

1. Have you ever walked through a season in which it seemed you
    would never make it out alive?
    - Are you walking through such a season now?
    - How was—or is—that season different from other hard
      circumstances in your life?

2. Flannery O'Connor, a southern writer who lived in the nineteen
    hundreds wrote, "All human nature vigorously resists grace because
    grace changes us and the change is painful."[44] Painful experiences
    in life are often amplified by the fact that they change or disrupt life
    as we know it and leave scars of change on us.
    - Has the hardest season of your life changed you? If so, how?
    - If you are walking through the "perfect" storm now, do you feel
      yourself changing, either positively or negatively? Explain.
    - Are you able to see those changes as a form of grace? Why or
      why not?

3. Sometimes our actions ignite the storms of life, and sometimes the
    storms seem capricious and random.

- Is there something you need to confess before you can cling to the grace of God in this storm?
- Is part of what you are experiencing a consequence of not listening to God's warnings?
- Or, if your season of trial feels capricious, is something keeping you from accepting the peace that God wants to offer?

4. Times of despair and anxiety are not one-night storms; they can last for years. Tragedy does not adhere to the rules of convenience. Following are two lines from the famous hymn "A Mighty Fortress Is Our God":

> A mighty fortress is our God, a bulwark never failing;
> Our helper He, amid the flood of mortal ills prevailing.[5]

Martin Luther (the writer of this hymn), Paul, Daniel, and countless others knew the only way to survive a "perfect storm," a season that throws change at you from every direction, is by having a bulwark.

- What is your bulwark? Do you have anything to hold on to during this season of change and insecurity when you hardly recognize yourself?
- Are there certain pillars you have turned to in the past that have crumbled under your weight?

CHOOSE CALM

5. Followers of Jesus know that he is their bulwark, but even more specifically the peace of God is a bulwark. It is steady and sure and a promise for those who believe in him.
- What might the peace of God feel like in your situation?

- Have you ever experienced it? If not, what do you think is the barrier to your peace?
- If you have not experienced it, do you still believe the peace of God exists?

6. Asking and not receiving can feel like rejection, and rejection on top of a tragic experience can seem unbearable. Can you relate to any of these questions?

    Have your prayers been met with a silent sky?

    Have you prayed and heard nothing?

    Are you floundering in the land between an offered and an answered prayer?

    Do you feel the press of Satan's mortar and pestle?

    If so, are you willing to continue pursuing answers in Christ?

    Consider the options. Is there any other way that seems more hopeful?

7. Read Isaiah 40:31.
- What might it mean to wait on the Lord in your situation?
- If the wait renewed your strength, would the wait be worth it?

8. In this chapter Max advises, "Lead with worship. Go first to your Father in prayer and praise. Confess to him your fears. Gather with his people. Set your face toward God. Fast. Cry out for help. Admit your weakness. Then, once God moves, you move too. Expect to see the God of ages fight for you. He is near, as near as your next breath."
- List the action items in this quote.
- Are you expecting God to move but not asking him to do so?
- Are you drowning in your depression without crying to him for help?
- How can you expect more of God in your situation?

- What do you need in order to be confident in his ownership of every second of your life?
- Read through chapter 8 again, noticing each example or story of how God held back the storm. Do you think the characters in those stories were confident their stories would end the way they did?

   Make a point to remind yourself of a different story from this chapter each day of this week.

MEDITATION

"When you have Him you have all; but you have also lost all when you lose Him. *Stay with Christ*, although your eyes do not see Him and your reason does not grasp Him."[6]

—MARTIN LUTHER, EMPHASIS ADDED

Chapter 9

THINK ABOUT WHAT
YOU THINK ABOUT

*Your problem is not your problem
but the way you see it.*

CONFRONT THE CHAOS

1. Consider this statement: "You didn't select your birthplace or birth date. You didn't choose your parents or siblings. You don't determine the weather or the amount of salt in the ocean. There are many things in life over which you have no choice. But the greatest activity of life is well within your dominion. You can choose what you think about."

   • Do you find it difficult to control what you think about?
   • Describe an experience when you felt you took control of your thoughts.

2. Do you let your mind wander?

   • Where does your mind go when you don't direct it?
   • How do you feel afterward?

3. We are bombarded every day with information that fights for our brain space (marketers are good at what they do!). Cell phones,

social media, and advertisements deliver a ceaseless deluge of content.

- What things do you indulge in even though you know you should stay away from them and keep your mind focused on truth? List those things.
- Why do you make these choices?
- What do you notice about your circumstances or physical state when you are more susceptible to letting down your mental guard?

4. Do you agree with this statement: "Your challenge is not your challenge. Your challenge is the way you think about your challenge. Your problem is not your problem; it is the way you look at it"?

- Why or why not?
- Fill in the blanks: My problem is not _____; it's the _____ I let my mind focus on.

CHOOSE CALM

5. Read Philippians 4:8–9 again and write down the attributes Paul encourages us to focus on. Particularly note the very first attribute Paul mentions.

- Is the source of your anxiety *true*?
- Has it become a reality, or is it something that *might* happen?
- If it hasn't happened, don't dwell on it!

6. On the other hand if the source of your anxiety is a reality, make a list of other *truths* that are good. These things are just as true as the mountain you face.

———•———

- Which list will you make a priority in your mind?
- How do you think the Holy Spirit plays a role in helping you do this?

7. Whom do you go to when you hear bad news? List at least three people.

   - Where is God on the list?
   - What does his position on this list say about your belief in his ability to solve your problems or his desire to hear your prayers?

8. Read Psalm 8 and Psalm 121.

   - Does anything about God strike you in these passages?
   - Often our view of our problems looms larger than our view of God. How can you start the day in a way that places the source of your anxiety in proper perspective relative to God's magnanimous power?

9. Take time to write down today's anxious thoughts in the form of bullet points, and bring each of them before the Lord with this prayer: "Jesus, this anxious, negative thought just wormed its way into my mind. Is it from you?" Ask Jesus to take away whatever thoughts are not from him.

MEDITATION

O God, early in the morning I cry to you.
Help me to pray and gather my thoughts to you,
   I cannot do it alone.
In me it is dark, but with you there is light;
I am lonely, but you do not desert me;
My courage fails me, but with you there is help;

———•———

I am restless, but with you there is peace;

in me there is bitterness, but with you there is patience;

I do not understand your ways, but you know the way for me.

Father in Heaven praise and thanks be to you for the night.[7]

—DIETRICH BONHOEFFER, A PRAYER

WRITTEN IN TEGEL PRISON, BERLIN

Chapter 10

CLING TO CHRIST

We bear fruit by focusing on God.

CONFRONT THE CHAOS

1. Our culture is characterized by a performance mentality. The focus is on results—at our jobs, in our athletic careers, in our hobbies. We want to know what something can be used for or what it produces.

   - Do you approach life with Jesus this way? How or how not?
   - Do you sometimes feel as if following Jesus is another burden? Why or why not?

2. After reading chapter 10, how *should* you be approaching a life of following Jesus?

3. While overcoming anxiety is important, another goal is mentioned in this chapter—one that speaks to our purpose here on earth, a reminder of the bigger picture. Did you pick up on it? Hint: Read John 15:8. Sometimes we need to declutter our spiritual to-do list.

   - Read Luke 10:39–42 and specifically note what Jesus says to Martha.
   - What does Jesus desire to see in us?
   - Combining John 15 and Luke 10, define the one overarching

goal for your life.

- Does it relieve your anxiety to know Jesus has a singular focus when he looks at your heart?

CHOOSE CALM

4. Philippians 4 holds several commands: "Be anxious for nothing," "With thanksgiving, let your requests be made known to God," "Rejoice in the Lord always," and the list goes on. Chances are, you want to do all these things. This sounds beautiful, but perhaps you are tired. Pain, loss, hurt, and anxiety may have worn you thin, and the thought of mustering enough strength to do these things, to live anxiety-free, is just not something you can take on.

Chapter 10 is an oasis in the desert. Instead of answering more questions, for the rest of this section consider the quotes and the scriptures below. Journal responses to them. Let them wash over you and bolster your strength. Use these passages to practice abiding in Christ.

"You grow weary of unrest. You're ready to be done with sleepless nights. You long to be 'anxious for nothing.' You long for the fruit of the Spirit. But how do you bear this fruit? Try harder? No, hang tighter. *Our assignment is not fruitfulness but faithfulness.* The secret to fruit bearing and anxiety-free living is *less about doing and more about abiding.*"

"Abide in Me, and I in you. As the branch cannot bear fruit of itself unless it abides in the vine, so neither can you unless you abide in Me. . . . he who abides in Me and I in him, he bears much fruit. . . . If anyone does not abide in Me, he is thrown away as a branch and dries up. . . . If you abide in Me, and My words abide in you, ask whatever you wish, and it will be done for you. . . . abide in My love . . . abide in My love; just as I have kept My Father's commandments and abide in His love" (John 15:4–10 NASB).

"Come, live in me!" Jesus invites. "Make my home your home."

"When a father leads his four-year-old son down a crowded street, he takes him by the hand and says, 'Hold on to me.' He doesn't say, 'Memorize the map' or 'Take your chances dodging the traffic' or 'Let's see if you can find your way home.' The good father gives the child one responsibility: 'Hold on to my hand.'

"God does the same with us. Don't load yourself down with lists. Don't enhance your anxiety with the fear of not fulfilling them. Your goal is not to know every detail of the future. Your goal is to hold the hand of the One who does and never, ever let go."

"Therefore I say to you, do not worry about your life, what you will eat or what you will drink; nor about your body, what you will put on. Is not life more than food and the body more than clothing? Look at the birds of the air, for they neither sow nor reap nor gather into barns; yet your heavenly Father feeds them. Are you not of more value than they? Which of you by worrying can add one cubit to his stature?

"So why do you worry about clothing? Consider the lilies of the field, how they grow: they neither toil nor spin; and yet I say to you that even Solomon in all his glory was not arrayed like one of these. Now if God so clothes the grass of the field, which today is, and tomorrow is thrown into the oven, will He not much more clothe you, O you of little faith?

"Therefore do not worry, saying, 'What shall we eat?' or 'What shall we drink?' or 'What shall we wear?' For after all these things the Gentiles seek. For your heavenly Father knows that you need all these things. But seek first the kingdom of God and His righteousness, and all these things shall be added to you. Therefore do not worry about tomorrow, for tomorrow will worry about its own things. Sufficient for the day is its own trouble" (Matt. 6:25–34).

MEDITATION

"As the Father has loved me, so have I loved you. Abide in my love. If you keep my commandments, you will abide in my love, just as I have kept my Father's commandments and abide in his love. These things I have spoken to you, that my joy may be in you, and that your joy may be full" (John 15:9–11 ESV).

Chapter 11

C.A.L.M.

Choose the tranquili-tree over the anxie-tree.

CONFRONT THE CHAOS

1. How has wrestling with anxiety shaped the way you view yourself? In chapter 11 Max asks, "What does all this anxiety mean?" How would you answer?

2. Before reading this chapter, had you ever considered that Jesus struggled with anxiety? Read Luke 22 and notice how Jesus walked through his most anxious moments on earth.

   - How does this change your perspective on your own struggle?
   - How does this change your perspective on the way God views your personal struggle with anxiety or depression?

3. Although Jesus was intimately acquainted with anxiety, he never let anxiety sway his purpose. He acknowledged it and brought it before his Father (Luke 22:42) but chose his actions based on predetermined will and logic. Hence, he walked to Calvary anyway.

   - Think about this past week. What decisions (large or small) did you make based on your anxiety? When did you let your fear choose for you? Be specific.
   - How might the outcomes of these situations have been different

———•———

if you had acknowledged your anxious thoughts but not given them power over your actions?

4. Do you truly believe that anxiety can be a part of your life without dominating your life?

   - Why or why not?
   - How do you currently deal with anxiety when it pops up?

CHOOSE CALM

5. "Rejoice in the Lord always. Again I will say, rejoice!" Paul encourages us to *celebrate God's goodness.*

   - What do you have to celebrate today?
   - What do you see around you that is lovely or worthy of praise?
   - What is the consequence on the "decision tree" of rejoicing?

6. "Be anxious for nothing, but in everything by prayer and supplication, with thanksgiving, let your requests be made known to God." Paul encourages us to *ask for God's help* and *leave our concerns with God.*

   - What do you want his help with today? He wants you to share *whatever* is on your heart. Nothing is too small or too large for him.
   - What do you need to leave (completely, not partially!) at his feet today?
   - What is the consequence of asking for help and leaving your concerns there?

7. "Finally, brethren, whatever things are true, whatever things are noble, whatever things are just, whatever things are pure, whatever things are lovely, whatever things are of good report, if there is any

virtue and if there is anything praiseworthy—meditate on these things." Paul encourages us to *meditate on good things*.

- What do you need to remove from your life to keep your mind focused on good things? What practices can you implement that will daily remind you of what is true, good, and beautiful?
- What is the consequence of meditating on the good things in this passage?

8. *Anxious for Nothing* ends with this statement: "A new day awaits you, my friend. A new season in which you will worry less and trust more. A season with reduced fear and enhanced faith. Can you imagine a life in which you are anxious for nothing? God can. And, with his help, you will experience it."

   Below is the resolve Max wrote. Take time to write your own—a commitment to yourself that you, too, will learn to live in the present and approach each day with a renewed sense of God's love for you and his deep care for the storms you walk through in this life.

MEDITATION

Today, I will live today.
Yesterday has passed.
Tomorrow is not yet.
I'm left with today.
So, today, I will live today.
Relive yesterday? No.
I will learn from it.
I will seek mercy for it.
I will take joy in it.
But I won't live in it.

The sun has set on yesterday.
The sun has yet to rise on tomorrow.
Worry about the future? To what gain?
It deserves a glance, nothing more.
I can't change tomorrow until tomorrow.
Today, I will live today.
I will face today's challenges with today's strength.
I will dance today's waltz with today's music.
I will celebrate today's opportunities with today's hope.
Today.

SCRIPTURES

Chapter 1: Less Fret, More Faith

Do not fret—it only causes harm.

—Psalm 37:8

Be anxious for nothing.

—Philippians 4:6

"Be careful, or your hearts will be weighed
down with . . . the anxieties of life."

—Luke 21:34 niv

Rejoice in the Lord always. Again I will say, rejoice! Let your gentleness be known to all men. The Lord is at hand. Be anxious for nothing, but in everything by prayer and supplication, with thanksgiving, let your requests be made known to God; and the peace of God, which surpasses all understanding, will guard your hearts and minds through Christ Jesus. Finally, brethren, whatever things are true, whatever things are noble, whatever things are just, whatever things are pure, whatever things are

---

lovely, whatever things are of good report, if there is any virtue
and if there is anything praiseworthy—meditate on these things.

—PHILIPPIANS 4:4–8

CHAPTER 2: REJOICE IN THE LORD'S SOVEREIGNTY

Rejoice in the Lord always. Again I will say, rejoice!

—PHILIPPIANS 4:4

The things which happened to me have actually turned out for the
furtherance of the gospel, so that it has become evident to the whole
palace guard, and to all the rest, that my chains are in Christ.

—PHILIPPIANS 1:12–13

Whether their motives are false or genuine, the
message about Christ is being preached either way,
so I rejoice. And I will continue to rejoice.

—PHILIPPIANS 1:18 NLT

God highly exalted [Jesus] and gave Him the
name that is above every name.

—PHILIPPIANS 2:9 HCSB

God . . . works in you both to will and to do for His good pleasure.

—PHILIPPIANS 2:13

There is no wisdom, no insight, no plan that
can succeed against the LORD.

—PROVERBS 21:30 NIV

[God] does as he pleases with the powers of heaven
and the peoples of the earth. No one can hold back
his hand or say to him: "What have you done?"

—Daniel 4:35 niv

[God] sustains all things.

—Hebrews 1:3 nrsv

[God can] whistle for the fly that is in the
farthest part of the rivers of Egypt.

—Isaiah 7:18

Who can act against you without the Lord's permission?
It is the Lord who helps one and harms another.

—Lamentations 3:37–38 tlb

"Holy, holy, holy, is the Lord of hosts;
The whole earth is full of His glory!"

—Isaiah 6:1–3

[He] is the Creator, who is blessed forever.

—Romans 1:25

[He] is the same yesterday, today, and forever.

—Hebrews 13:8

[His] years will never end.

—Psalm 102:27 niv

My soul has been rejected from peace;
I have forgotten happiness.
So I say, "My strength has perished,
And so has my hope from the LORD."
Remember my affliction and my wandering,
the wormwood and bitterness.
Surely my soul remembers
And is bowed down within me.
This I recall to my mind,
Therefore I have hope.
The LORD's lovingkindnesses indeed never cease,
For His compassions never fail.
They are new every morning;
Great is Your faithfulness.
"The LORD is my portion," says my soul,
"Therefore I have hope in Him."
The LORD is good to those who wait for Him,
To the person who seeks Him.
It is good that he waits silently
For the salvation of the LORD.

—LAMENTATIONS 3:17–26 NASB

In everything God works for the good
of those who love him.

—ROMANS 8:28 NCV

He will keep in perfect peace all those who trust in
him, whose thoughts turn often to the Lord!

—ISAIAH 26:3 TLB

———•———

CHAPTER 3: REJOICE IN THE LORD'S MERCY

When I refused to confess my sin,
my body wasted away,
and I groaned all day long.
Day and night your hand of discipline was heavy on me.
My strength evaporated like water in the summer heat.

—PSALM 32:3–4 NLT

If anyone ever had reason to hope that he could save himself, it would be I [Paul]. If others could be saved by what they are, certainly I could! For I went through the Jewish initiation ceremony when I was eight days old, having been born into a pure-blooded Jewish home that was a branch of the old original Benjamin family. So I was a real Jew if there ever was one! What's more, I was a member of the Pharisees who demand the strictest obedience to every Jewish law and custom. And sincere? Yes, so much so that I greatly persecuted the Church; and I tried to obey every Jewish rule and regulation right down to the very last point. But all these things that I once thought very worthwhile—now I've thrown them all away so that I can put my trust and hope in Christ alone.

—PHILIPPIANS 3:4–7 TLB

I [Paul] am right with God, not because I followed
the law, but because I believed in Christ.

—PHILIPPIANS 3:9 NCV

I [Paul] am still not all I should be, but I am bringing all my energies to bear on this one thing: Forgetting the past and

looking forward to what lies ahead, I strain to reach the end
of the race and receive the prize for which God is calling us
up to heaven because of what Christ Jesus did for us.

—PHILIPPIANS 3:13–14 TLB

God's readiness to give and forgive is now
public. Salvation's available for everyone! . . . Tell
them all this. Build up their courage.

—TITUS 2:11, 15 THE MESSAGE

Forgetting the past and looking forward to what
lies ahead, I strain to reach the end of the race and
receive the prize for which God is calling us.

—PHILIPPIANS 3:13–14 TLB

And *I know* the Lord will continue to rescue me from every *trip,
trap, snare, and pitfall of* evil and carry me safely to His heavenly
kingdom. May He be glorified throughout eternity. Amen.

—2 TIMOTHY 4:18 THE VOICE

CHAPTER 4: REJOICE IN
THE LORD *ALWAYS*

The Son is the radiance of God's glory and the exact representation of his being, sustaining all things by his powerful word.

—HEBREWS 1:3 NIV

He is before all things, and in him all things hold together.

—COLOSSIANS 1:17 NIV

————•————

"For in him we live and move and have our being."

—Acts 17:28 NIV

[He] works out everything in conformity with the purpose of his will.

—Ephesians 1:11 NIV

He makes grass grow for the cattle,
and plants for people to cultivate—
bringing forth food from the earth:
wine that gladdens human hearts,
oil to make their faces shine,
and bread that sustains their hearts.

—Psalm 104:14–15 NIV

"[God] causes his sun to rise on the evil and the good, and
sends rain on the righteous and the unrighteous."

—Matthew 5:45 NIV

The Most High God rules the kingdom of
men, and sets over it whom he will.

—Daniel 5:21 RSV

It is God who executes judgment,
putting down one and lifting up another.

—Psalm 75:7 NRSV

The fierce anger of the LORD will not turn back until he has
executed and accomplished the intents of his mind.

—Jeremiah 30:24 NRSV

In him we were also chosen, . . . according to the plan of him who
works out everything in conformity with the purpose of his will.

—Ephesians 1:11 niv

"You intended to harm me, but God intended it for good to
accomplish what is now being done, the saving of many lives. So
then, don't be afraid. I will provide for you and your children."

—Genesis 50:20–21 niv

"This man was handed over to you by God's deliberate plan
and foreknowledge; and you, with the help of wicked men, put
him to death by nailing him to the cross. *But God* raised him
from the dead, freeing him from the agony of death, because
it was impossible for death to keep its hold on him."

—Acts 2:23–24 niv, emphasis mine

In all things God works for the good of those who love
him, who have been called according to his purpose.

—Romans 8:28 niv

Chapter 5: Contagious Calm

Let your gentleness be evident to all. The Lord is
near. Do not be anxious about anything.

—Philippians 4:5–6 niv

"Do not be afraid. . . . I am your shield, your
exceedingly great reward."

—Genesis 15:1

"Do not be afraid, for I am with you.

—Genesis 26:24 nlt

Do not be afraid; do not be discouraged, for the Lord
your God will be with you wherever you go."

—Joshua 1:9 niv

The Lord is with me; I will not be afraid.
What can mere mortals do to me?

—Psalm 118:6 niv

Jesus lifted up His eyes, and seeing a great multitude
coming toward Him, He said to Philip, "Where shall we
buy bread, that these may eat?" But this He said to test
him, for He Himself knew what He would do.

—John 6:5–6

"Send the multitudes away, that they may go into
the villages and buy themselves food."

—Matthew 14:15

Jesus said, "Have the people sit down." There was plenty of
grass in that place, and they sat down (about five thousand
men were there). Jesus then took the loaves, gave thanks,
and distributed to those who were seated as much as they
wanted. He did the same with the fish. When they had
all had enough to eat, he said to his disciples, "Gather the
pieces that are left over. Let nothing be wasted." So they
gathered them and filled twelve baskets with the pieces of

the five barley loaves left over by those who had eaten.

—John 6:10–13 niv

Chapter 6: Prayer, Not Despair

"Don't you think God will surely give justice to his chosen people who cry out to him day and night? . . . I
tell you, he will grant justice to them quickly!"

—Luke 18: 7–8 nlt

Be anxious for nothing, but in everything by
prayer and supplication, with thanksgiving, let
your requests be made known to God.

—Philippians 4:6

Cast all your anxiety on him because he cares for you.

—1 Peter 5:7 niv

Put the Lord in remembrance [of His promises],
keep not silence.

—Isaiah 62:6 ampc

"Put Me in remembrance;
Let us contend together."

—Isaiah 43:26

You said you would walk me through the waters.

—Isaiah 43:2, author's paraphrase

———•———

You said you would lead me through the valley.

—PSALM 23:4, AUTHOR'S PARAPHRASE

You said that you would never leave or forsake me.

—HEBREWS 13:5, AUTHOR'S PARAPHRASE

Prayer is essential in this ongoing warfare. Pray hard
and long. Pray for your brothers and sisters.

—EPHESIANS 6:18 THE MESSAGE

CHAPTER 7: GREAT GRATITUDE

Be anxious for nothing, but in everything by prayer and supplication, with thanksgiving, let your requests be made known
to God; and the peace of God, which surpasses all understanding, will guard your hearts and minds through Christ Jesus.

—PHILIPPIANS 4:6–7

I have learned to be content whatever the circumstances.
I know what it is to be in need, and I know what it
is to have plenty. I have learned the secret of being
content in any and every situation, whether well fed
or hungry, whether living in plenty or in want. I can
do all this through him who gives me strength.

—PHILIPPIANS 4:11–13 NIV

I have learned the secret of being content—whether well
fed or hungry, whether in abundance or in need.

—PHILIPPIANS 4:12 HCSB

To me the only important thing about living is
Christ, and dying would be profit for me.

—PHILIPPIANS 1:21 NCV

CHAPTER 8: GOD'S PEACE, YOUR PEACE

The peace of God, which surpasses all understanding, will
guard your hearts and minds through Christ Jesus.

—PHILIPPIANS 4:7

"Peace I leave with you; my peace I give you. I do
not give to you as the world gives. Do not let your
hearts be troubled and do not be afraid."

—JOHN 14:27 NIV

All the angels are spirits who serve God and are sent
to help those who will receive salvation.

—HEBREWS 1:14 NCV

"Since the first day that you set your mind to
gain understanding and to humble yourself
before your God, your words were heard."

—DANIEL 10:12 NIV

"I will contend with him who contends with you."

—ISAIAH 49:25

Those who wait on the LORD
Shall renew their strength;

They shall mount up with wings like eagles,
They shall run and not be weary,
They shall walk and not faint.

—ISAIAH 40:31

He [God] has put his angels in charge of you
to watch over you wherever you go.

—PSALM 91:11 NCV

"I am the good shepherd; I know my
sheep and my sheep know me."

—JOHN 10:14 NIV

You are no longer a slave but God's own child. And since
you are his child, God has made you his heir.

—GALATIANS 4:7 NLT

"For there stood by me this night an angel of the
God to whom I belong and whom I serve."

—ACTS 27:23

All the days planned for me
were written in your book
before I was one day old.

—PSALM 139:16 NCV

"In this world you will have trouble, but be
brave! I have defeated the world."

—JOHN 16:33 NCV

"Do not be afraid nor dismayed because of this great
multitude, for the battle is not yours, but God's."

—2 Chronicles 20:15

"When you pass through the waters, I will be with you."

—Isaiah 43:2 niv

Chapter 9: Think About What You Think About

Be careful what you think,
because your thoughts run your life.

—Proverbs 4:23 ncv

Fix your thoughts on what is true, and honorable, and
right, and pure, and lovely, and admirable. Think about
things that are excellent and worthy of praise.

—Philippians 4:8 nlt

Anxiety weighs down the human heart.

—Proverbs 12:25 nrsv

Capture every thought and make it
give up and obey Christ.

—2 Corinthians 10:5 ncv

Fasten the belt of truth around your waist.

—Ephesians 6:14 nrsv

—•—

O my soul, bless GOD,
don't forget a single blessing!

—PSALM 103:2 THE MESSAGE

CHAPTER 10: CLING TO CHRIST

Fix your thoughts on what is true, and honorable, and
right, and pure, and lovely, and admirable. Think about
things that are excellent and worthy of praise.

—PHILIPPIANS 4:8 NLT

"Abide in Me, and I in you. As the branch cannot bear fruit of itself
unless it abides in the vine, so neither can you unless you abide in
Me. I am the vine, you are the branches; he who abides in Me and
I in him, he bears much fruit, for apart from Me you can do nothing. If anyone does not abide in Me, he is thrown away as a branch
and dries up; and they gather them, and cast them into the fire and
they are burned. If you abide in Me, and My words abide in you, ask
whatever you wish, and it will be done for you. My Father is glorified
by this, that you bear much fruit, and so prove to be My disciples.
Just as the Father has loved Me, I have also loved you; abide in My
love. If you keep My commandments, you will abide in My love; just
as I have kept My Father's commandments and abide in His love."

—JOHN 15:4–10 NASB

"Do not worry about your life, what you will eat or what you
will drink; nor about your body, what you will put on. . . .
Look at the birds of the air, for they neither sow nor reap nor

gather into barns; yet your heavenly Father feeds them. Are you not of more value than they? Which of you by worrying can add one cubit to his stature? . . . Consider the lilies . . . even Solomon . . . was not arrayed like one of these."

—MATTHEW 6:25–29

Set your mind on things above, not on things on the earth.

—COLOSSIANS 3:2

"If you abide in my word, you are truly my disciples, and you will know the truth, and the truth will set you free."

—JOHN 8:31–32 ESV

CHAPTER 11: C.A.L.M.

Rejoice in the Lord always. Again I will say, rejoice! Let your gentleness be known to all men. The Lord is at hand. Be anxious for nothing, but in everything by prayer and supplication, with thanksgiving, let your requests be made known to God; and the peace of God, which surpasses all understanding, will guard your hearts and minds through Christ Jesus. Finally, brethren, whatever things are true, whatever things are noble, whatever things are just, whatever things are pure, whatever things are lovely, whatever things are of good report, if there is any vir- tue and if there is anything praiseworthy—meditate on these things.

—PHILIPPIANS 4:4–8

"Be careful. Be calm and don't worry."

—ISAIAH 7:4 NCV

Rejoice in the Lord always. Again I will say, rejoice!

—Philippians 4:4

I will lift up my eyes to the hills—
From whence comes my help?
My help comes from the Lord,
Who made heaven and earth.

—Psalm 121:1–2

Peter said, "Lord, if it is really you, then command
me to come to you on the water."

Jesus said, "Come."

And Peter left the boat and walked on the water to Jesus.
But when Peter saw the wind and the waves, he became
afraid and began to sink. He shouted, "Lord, save me!"

—Matthew 14:28–30 ncv

God . . . is the blessed controller of all things, the king
over all kings and the master of all masters.

—1 Timothy 6:15 phillips

There is now no condemnation for
those who are in Christ Jesus.

—Romans 8:1 niv

Let your requests be made known to God.

—Philippians 4:6

"Call on me in the day of trouble."

—PSALM 50:15 NIV

"Ask, and it will be given to you; seek, and you will
find; knock, and it will be opened to you."

—MATTHEW 7:7

Let us then approach God's throne of grace with confidence.

—HEBREWS 4:16 NIV

Guard your hearts and minds through Christ Jesus.

—PHILIPPIANS 4:7

I know whom I have believed and am persuaded that He is
able to keep what I have committed to Him until that Day.

—2 TIMOTHY 1:12

Finally, brethren, whatever things are true, whatever things are noble,
whatever things are just, whatever things are pure, whatever things
are lovely, whatever things are of good report, if there is any virtue
and if there is anything praiseworthy—meditate on these things.

—PHILIPPIANS 4:8

NOTES

CHAPTER 1: LESS FRET, MORE FAITH

1. *Haole* (pronounced HOW-leh) is a Hawaiian word for nonnatives, particularly white people. One definition comes from *ha*, meaning "breath" or "spirit," and *ole*, meaning "none" or "without." Some believe the term originated when the Christian missionaries first came to the islands. Kapehu Retreat House, "Hawaiian Words," www.kapehu.com /hawaiian-words.html.

2. Edmund J. Bourne, *The Anxiety and Phobia Workbook*, 5th ed. (Oakland, CA: New Harbinger, 2010), xi.

3. Taylor Clark, "It's Not the Job Market: The Three Real Reasons Why Americans Are More Anxious Than Ever Before," *Slate*, January 31, 2011, http://www.slate.com/articles/arts/culturebox/2011/01/its_not_the_job _market.html.

4. Ibid.

5. John Ortberg, *Soul Keeping: Caring for the Most Important Part of You* (Grand Rapids, MI: Zondervan, 2014), 46.

6. Clark, "It's Not the Job Market."

7. Ibid.

8. Robert L. Leahy, *Anxiety Free: Unravel Your Fears Before They Unravel You* (Carlsbad, CA: Hay House, 2009), 4.

9. Bourne, *The Anxiety and Phobia Workbook*, xi.

10. Joel J. Miller, "The Secret Behind the Bible's Most Highlighted Verse,"

Theology That Sticks (blog), AncientFaith.com, August 24, 2015, https://blogs.ancientfaith.com/joeljmiller/bibles-most-highlighted-verse/.

CHAPTER 2: REJOICE IN THE LORD'S SOVEREIGNTY

1. John MacArthur Jr., *Philippians*, The MacArthur New Testament Commentary (Chicago: Moody Press, 2001), 273.
2. Taylor Clark, *Nerve: Poise Under Pressure, Serenity Under Stress, and the Brave New Science of Fear and Cool* (New York: Little, Brown, 2011), 100–101.
3. Ibid.
4. Alan Mozes, "Traffic Jams Harm the Heart," HealthDay, March 13, 2009, https://consumer.healthday.com/cardiovascular-and-health-information -20/heart-attack-news-357/traffic-jams-harm-the-heart-624998.html.

CHAPTER 3: REJOICE IN THE LORD'S MERCY

1. Used with permission.
2. Henri J. M. Nouwen, *The Essential Henri Nouwen*, ed. Robert A. Jonas (Boston: Shambhala, 2009), 131–32.

CHAPTER 4: REJOICE IN THE LORD *ALWAYS*

1. Taylor Clark, *Nerve: Poise Under Pressure, Serenity Under Stress, and the Brave New Science of Fear and Cool* (New York: Little, Brown, 2011), 25–26.
2. Spiros Zodhiates, ed., *Hebrew-Greek Key Word Study Bible: Key Insights into God's Word, New International Version* (Chattanooga, TN: AMG Publishers, 1996), #5770, 2122.
3. Ibid., #1919, 2072.
4. L. B. Cowman, *Streams in the Desert: 366 Daily Devotional Readings,* ed. Jim Reimann, updated ed. (Grand Rapids, MI: Zondervan, 1997), 462–63.
5. "Telegram from Anna Spafford to Horatio Gates Spafford re Being 'Saved Alone' Among Her Traveling Party in the Shipwreck of the Ville du Havre," Library of Congress, https://www.loc.gov/item/mamcol000006.
6. Horatio Spafford, "It Is Well with My Soul," CyberHymnal.org, http://cyberhymnal.org/htm/i/t/i/itiswell.htm.

CHAPTER 5: CONTAGIOUS CALM

1. Taylor Clark, *Nerve: Poise Under Pressure, Serenity Under Stress, and the Brave New Science of Fear and Cool* (New York: Little, Brown, 2011), 3–9.

2. Gerhard Kittel, ed., *Theological Dictionary of the New Testament,* trans. and ed. Geoffrey W. Bromiley (Grand Rapids, MI: Wm. B. Eerdmans, 1964), 2:588–89.

3. W. E. Vine, *Vine's Expository Dictionary of New Testament Words: A Comprehensive Dictionary of the Original Greek Words with Their Precise Meanings for English Readers* (McLean, VA: MacDonald Publishing, n.d.), "Gentle, Gentleness, Gently," 484–85.

4. John Chrysostom, *Homilies on Paul's Letter to the Philippians*, trans. Pauline Allen (Atlanta, GA: Society of Biblical Literature, 2013), 285.

5. *Theodoret of Cyrus: Commentary on the Letters of St Paul*, trans. Robert Charles Hill (Brookline, MA: Holy Cross Orthodox Press, 2001), 2:78.

6. William C. Frey, *The Dance of Hope: Finding Ourselves in the Rhythm of God's Great Story* (Colorado Springs, CO: WaterBrook Press, 2003), 175.

CHAPTER 7: GREAT GRATITUDE

1. Kennon M. Sheldon, Todd B. Kashdan, and Michael F. Steger, eds., *Designing Positive Psychology: Taking Stock and Moving Forward* (New York: Oxford University Press, 2011), 249–54. See also Amit Amin, "The 31 Benefits of Gratitude You Didn't Know About: How Gratitude Can Change Your Life," Happier Human, http://happierhuman.com /benefits-of-gratitude/.

CHAPTER 8: GOD'S PEACE, YOUR PEACE

1. Martin Luther, "A Mighty Fortress Is Our God," trans. Frederic H. Hedge, http://cyberhymnal.org/htm/m/i/mightyfo.htm.

2. John B. Polhill, *Acts,* vol. 26, *The New American Commentary*, ed. David S. Dockery (Nashville, TN: Broadman and Holman, 1992), 517.

3. William J. Larkin Jr., *Acts,* The IVP New Testament Commentary Series, ed. Grant R. Osborne (Downers Grove, IL: InterVarsity Press, 1995), 369.

4. Darrell L. Bock, *Acts,* Baker Exegetical Commentary on the New Testament, eds. Robert W. Yarbrough and Robert H. Stein (Grand Rapids, MI: Baker Academic, 2007), 747.

5. For example, the English Standard Version, New International Version, New Living Translation, and The Message.

6. Story related to me in person. Used with permission.

CHAPTER 9: THINK ABOUT WHAT YOU THINK ABOUT

1. Used with permission.
2. Used with permission.

CHAPTER 10: CLING TO CHRIST

1. Kent and Amber Brantly with David Thomas, *Called for Life: How Loving Our Neighbor Led Us into the Heart of the Ebola Epidemic* (Colorado Springs, CO: WaterBrook, 2015), 97.
2. Hebrews 4:16 NIV, 1984 edition.
3. Brantly, *Called for Life*, 97.
4. Thomas Obediah Chisholm, "Great Is Thy Faithfulness," hymnal.net, https://www.hymnal.net/en/hymn/h/19.
5. Annie S. Hawks, "I Need Thee Every Hour," http://cyberhymnal.org /htm/i/n/ineedteh.htm.
6. Brantly, *Called for Life*, 115.

CHAPTER 11: C.A.L.M.

1. Spiros Zodhiates, ed., *Hebrew-Greek Key Word Study Bible: Key Insights into God's Word, New International Version* (Chattanooga, TN: AMG Publishers, 1996), #3534, p. 2093.

QUESTIONS FOR REFLECTION

1. Anonymous, "The Prayer of St. Patrick," Beliefnet, http://www.beliefnet .com/prayers/catholic/morning/the-prayer-of-st-patrick.aspx.
2. 2 Timothy 4:18 THE VOICE.
3. Horatio G. Spafford, "It Is Well with My Soul," Timeless Truths, http:// library.timelesstruths.org/music/It_Is_Well_with_My_Soul/.
4. Flannery O'Connor, *The Habit of Being: Letters of Flannery O'Connor*, ed. Sally Fitzgerald (New York: Farrar, Straus and Giroux, 1979), 307.
5. Martin Luther, "A Mighty Fortress Is Our God," Timeless Truths, http:// library.timelesstruths.org/music/A_Mighty_Fortress_Is_Our_God/.
6. Martin Luther, Billy Graham Center Museum, Wheaton College, http:// www.wheaton.edu/bgcmuseum/Exhibits/Rotunda-of-Witnesses /Martin-Luther.
7. Dietrich Bonhoeffer, "Dietrich Bonhoeffer's Prayer from Prison . . . ," *bonhoefferblog*, https://bonhoefferblog.wordpress.com/category/prayer/.

The Lucado Reader's Guide

Discover . . . Inside every book by Max Lucado, you'll find words of
encouragement and inspiration that will draw you into a deeper experience with
Jesus and treasures for your walk with God. What will you discover?

3:16: The Numbers of Hope
. . . the 26 words that can change
your life.
core scripture: John 3:16

And the Angels Were Silent
. . . what Jesus Christ's final days can
teach you about what matters most.
core scripture: Matthew 20–27

Anxious for Nothing
. . . be anxious for nothing.
core scripture: Philippians 4:4–8

The Applause of Heaven
. . . the secret to a truly satisfying life.
core scripture: The Beatitudes,
Matthew 5:1–10

Before Amen
. . . the power of a simple prayer.
core scripture: Psalm 145:19

Come Thirsty
. . . how to rehydrate your heart
and sink into the wellspring of
God's love.
core scripture: John 7:37–38

Cure for the Common Life
. . . the unique things God designed
you to do with your life.
core scripture: 1 Corinthians 12:7

Facing Your Giants
. . . when God is for you,
no challenge is too great.
core scripture: 1 and 2 Samuel

Fearless
. . . how faith is the antidote to
the fear in your life.
core scripture: John 14:1, 3

A Gentle Thunder
. . . the God who will do whatever it
takes to lead his children back to him.
core scripture: Psalm 81:7

Glory Days
. . . how you fight from victory,
not for it.
core scripture: Joshua 21:43–45

God Came Near
. . . a love so great that it left heaven
to become part of your world.
core scripture: John 1:14

Grace
. . . the incredible gift that saves
and sustains you.
core scripture: Hebrews 12:15

The Great House of God
. . . a blueprint for peace, joy, and
love found in the Lord's Prayer.
core scripture: The Lord's Prayer,
Matthew 6:9–13

He Chose the Nails
. . . a love so deep that it chose death
on a cross—just to win your heart.
core scripture: 1 Peter 1:18–20

He Still Moves Stones
. . . the God who still does the
impossible—in your life.
core scripture: Matthew 12:20

In the Eye of the Storm
. . . peace in the storms of your life.
core scripture: John 6

In the Grip of Grace
. . . the greatest gift of all—the
grace of God.
core scripture: Romans

It's Not About Me
. . . why focusing on God will make
sense of your life.
core scripture: 2 Corinthians 3:18

Just Like Jesus
. . . a life free from guilt, fear,
and anxiety.
core scripture: Ephesians 4:23–24

A Love Worth Giving
. . . how living loved frees you
to love others.
core scripture: 1 Corinthians 13

Next Door Savior
. . . a God who walked life's
hardest trials—and still walks
with you through yours.
core scripture: Matthew 16:13–16

**No Wonder They Call Him
the Savior**
. . . hope in the unlikeliest place—
upon the cross.
core scripture: Romans 5:15

Outlive Your Life
. . . that a great God created you
to do great things.
core scripture: Acts 1

Six Hours One Friday
. . . forgiveness and healing in
the middle of loss and failure.
core scripture: John 19–20

Traveling Light
. . . the power to release the burdens
you were never meant to carry.
core scripture: Psalm 23

Unshakable Hope
. . . God has given us his very great and
precious promises.
core scripture: 2 Peter 1:4

**When God Whispers
Your Name**
. . . the path to hope in knowing that
God knows you, never forgets you, and
cares about the details of your life.
core scripture: John 10:3

You'll Get Through This
. . . hope in the midst of your hard
times and a God who uses the mess
of life for good.
core scripture: Genesis 50:20

Recommended reading if you're struggling with . . .

FEAR AND WORRY

Anxious for Nothing
Before Amen
Come Thirsty
Fearless
For the Tough Times
Next Door Savior
Traveling Light

DISCOURAGEMENT

He Still Moves Stones
Next Door Savior

GRIEF/DEATH OF A LOVED ONE

Next Door Savior
Traveling Light
When Christ Comes
When God Whispers Your Name
You'll Get Through This

GUILT

In the Grip of Grace
Just Like Jesus

LONELINESS

God Came Near

SIN

Before Amen
Facing Your Giants
He Chose the Nails
Six Hours One Friday

WEARINESS

Before Amen
When God Whispers Your Name
You'll Get Through This

Recommended reading if you want to know more about . . .

THE CROSS

And the Angels Were Silent
He Chose the Nails
No Wonder They Call Him the Savior
Six Hours One Friday

GRACE

Before Amen
Grace
He Chose the Nails
In the Grip of Grace

HEAVEN

The Applause of Heaven
When Christ Comes

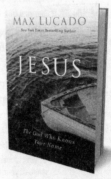

SHARING THE GOSPEL

God Came Near
Grace
No Wonder They Call Him the Savior

Recommended reading if you're looking for more . . .

COMFORT

For the Tough Times
He Chose the Nails
Next Door Savior
Traveling Light
You'll Get Through This

COMPASSION

Outlive Your Life

COURAGE

Facing Your Giants
Fearless

HOPE

3:16: The Numbers of Hope
Before Amen
Facing Your Giants
A Gentle Thunder
God Came Near
Grace
Unshakable Hope

JOY

The Applause of Heaven
Cure for the Common Life
When God Whispers Your Name

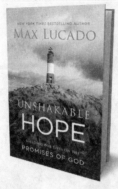

LOVE

Come Thirsty
A Love Worth Giving
No Wonder They Call Him the Savior

PEACE

And the Angels Were Silent
Anxious for Nothing
Before Amen
The Great House of God
In the Eye of the Storm
Traveling Light
You'll Get Through This

SATISFACTION

And the Angels Were Silent
Come Thirsty
Cure for the Common Life
Great Day Every Day

TRUST

A Gentle Thunder
It's Not About Me
Next Door Savior

Max Lucado books make great gifts!

If you're coming up to a special occasion, consider one of these.

FOR ADULTS:

Anxious for Nothing
For the Tough Times
Grace for the Moment
Live Loved
The Lucado Life Lessons Study Bible
Mocha with Max
DaySpring Daybrighteners® and cards

FOR TEENS/GRADUATES:

Let the Journey Begin
You Can Be Everything God Wants You to Be
You Were Made to Make a Difference

FOR KIDS:

I'm Not a Scaredy Cat
Just in Case You Ever Wonder
The Oak Inside the Acorn
You Are Special

FOR PASTORS AND TEACHERS:

God Thinks You're Wonderful
You Changed My Life

AT CHRISTMAS:

Because of Bethlehem
The Crippled Lamb
The Christmas Candle
God Came Near

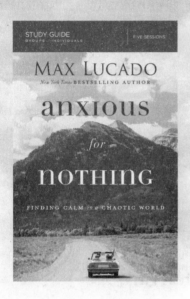
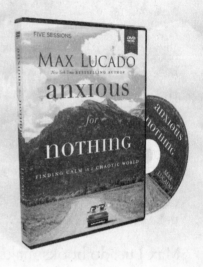

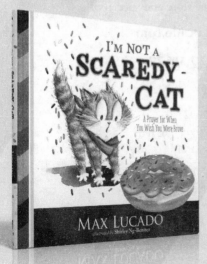